{ Knit It! Felt It!™ }

EDITED BY BOBBIE MATELA

HOUSE of
WHITE
BIRCHES

PUBLISHERS
SINCE 1947

Knit It! Felt It!™

EDITOR	Bobbie Matela
ART DIRECTOR	Brad Snow
PUBLISHING SERVICES MANAGER	Brenda Gallmeyer
SENIOR EDITOR	Kathy Wesley
ASSOCIATE EDITORS	Mary Ann Frits, Cathy Reef, Beth Camera
ASSISTANT ART DIRECTOR	Nick Pierce
COPY SUPERVISOR	Michelle Beck
COPY EDITORS	Mary O'Donnell, Kim English
TECHNICAL EDITOR	Charlotte Quiggle
GRAPHIC ARTS SUPERVISOR	Ronda Bechinski
GRAPHIC ARTISTS	Jessi Butler, Minette Collins Smith
PRODUCTION ASSISTANTS	Marj Morgan, Judy Neuenschwander
TECHNICAL ARTIST	Nicole Gage
PHOTOGRAPHY SUPERVISOR	Tammy Christian
PHOTOGRAPHY	Don Clark, Matthew Owen, Jackie Schaffel
PHOTO STYLISTS	Tammy Nussbaum, Tammy M. Smith
CHIEF EXECUTIVE OFFICER	David J. McKee
MARKETING VICE PRESIDENT	Dan Fink
EDITORIAL DIRECTOR	Jeanne Stauffer

Printed in the U.S.A.
First Printing in China: 2007
Softcover ISBN: 978-1-59217-156-9
Hardcover ISBN: 978-1-59217-151-4
Library of Congress Control Number: 2006928181

2 3 4 5 6 7 8 9

Welcome

You'll love the mystery, anticipation and the final finished felted projects that you create.

The stitches are formed loosely and quickly so that the fibers can agitate and produce enough friction to become felted. So while you are knitting, you are not exactly sure what your results will be. Each ball of yarn and every washing machine felts a little differently than the next. We enjoy the way each project becomes its own unique creation.

How will you decide what to knit from this exhilarating mix of over 60 projects? Start at the Top and choose from warm hats and scarves. Ensure Warm Hands this winter with colorful options for felted mittens. You'll enjoy Cozy Feet when you slip them into warm felted slippers. Our varied collection of Great Carriers makes it easy to find your signature purse or tote-bag style. Say you care with a felted gift from our Neat Conveniences chapter. Choose from an array of Stylish Living ideas to accessorize your home. Our designers have achieved true artistry with wool, alpaca and mohair from Plymouth Yarn Co. We're sure you will be inspired by their offerings.

With warm thoughts,

Bobbie Matela

Contents

Start at the Top: Hats & Scarves

Warm Hands: Mittens & Wristers

Cozy Feet: Slippers

Great Carriers: Purses & Totes

Neat Conveniences: Gifts & Things

Stylish Living: Vases, Pillows & More

Start at the Top: Hats & Scarves

FIND COLORFUL SHAPES AND PATTERNS AND CREATE FASHIONABLY WARM HATS, SCARVES OR A WINTER HEADBAND.

Fair Isle Hat

THE WARM COLORS OF THIS HAT WILL REMIND YOU THAT SPRING IS JUST AROUND THE CORNER, EVEN ON THE COLDEST WINTRY DAY.

DESIGN BY GAYLE BUNN

INTERMEDIATE

Size
Woman's average

Finished Felted Measurement
Circumference: Approx 22 inches
Measurement achieved using yarn and colors specified; results may vary depending on yarn, yarn color and felting time.

Materials
- Plymouth Suri Merino 55 percent suri alpaca/45 percent merino wool medium weight yarn (109 yds/50g per ball): 1 ball each tan #208 (MC), white #100 (A), pink #1970 (B), and light green #1310 (C)
- 4 yards of acrylic yarn (must be yarn which will not felt) in shade to match B
- Size 7 (4.5mm) 24-inch circular needle or size needed to obtain gauge
- Tapestry needle

Pre-Felted Gauge
20 sts and 26 rnds = 4 inches/10cm in stranded St st
To save time, take time to check gauge.

Hat
Using cable cast-on method, *cast on 1 st MC, cast on 1 st A; rep from * 63 times. (128 sts)
Cut A.
Join without twisting; pm between first and last sts.

With MC, knit 1 rnd.
Work 7 rnds of k2, p2 rib.
Work Rnds 1–49 of Chart on page 32; work Rnds 34–49.
Thread 2 strands of acrylic yarn through all sts on needle. Do not gather. Tie acrylic yarn ends tog securely.
Weave in yarn ends.

Pompom
With B, cast on 18 sts.
Work 3½ inches in St st.
Bind off.
Thread acrylic yarn through loops around outer edge of pompom. Do not gather.
Tie acrylic yarn ends tog securely.

CONTINUED ON PAGE 32

Ruffles on the Edge

PINK RUFFLES AND BEADS CREATE A FEMININE HAT FOR EITHER THE BIG OR LITTLE "LADY OF THE HOUSE."

DESIGN BY DONNA DRUCHUNAS

EASY

Sizes

Child (adult) Instructions are given for smaller size, with larger size in parentheses. When only 1 number is given, it applies to both sizes.

Finished Felted Measurement

Circumference: Approx 18 (21) inches

Measurement achieved using yarn and color specified; results may vary depending on yarn, yarn color and felting time.

Materials

- Plymouth Baby Alpaca Grande 100 percent baby alpaca bulky yarn (110 yds/100g per ball): 1 (2) balls pink #567
- Size 15 (10mm) 16-inch circular and double-pointed needles or size needed to obtain gauge
- Stitch markers
- 16 assorted beads
- Sewing needle and matching thread, or washable fabric glue

Pre-Felted Gauge

8 sts and 11 rows = 4 inches/10cm in St st

Exact gauge is not critical; make sure your sts are loose and airy.

Pattern Note

Change to dpns when sts no longer fit comfortably on circular needle.

Hat

Ruffle

With circular needle, cast on 200 (240) sts. Join without twisting; place marker between first and last sts.

Rnds 1, 3 and 5: Knit.
Rnd 2: K2tog around. (100, 120 sts)
Rnd 4: K2tog around. (50, 60 sts)

Sides

Knit every rnd until hat measures 8½ (11) inches from top of ruffle.

Crown

Rnd 1: *K8, k2tog, place marker; rep from * around. (45, 54 sts)
Rnd 2 and all even rounds: Knit.
Dec rnd: *Knit to 2 sts before marker, k2tog; rep from * around.
Rep Dec rnd every other rnd until 15 (18) sts rem.

Next rnd: *K2tog; rep from * around, end k1 (0). (8, 9 sts)
Cut yarn, leaving a 6-inch tail.
Thread the tail through the rem sts, pull tight and secure.
Weave in ends.

Felting

Follow basic felting instructions on page 168 until hat is just slightly smaller than finished measurements or desired size.

Block by stretching over a bowl that is just slightly larger than desired head size, or a hat form.

Finishing

Using the photo as a guide, sew or glue beads around hat just above ruffle. ✽

Just Like Mom

THESE CLOSE-FITTING HATS CAN ACTUALLY KEEP EVERYONE IN THE FAMILY WARM.

DESIGNS BY SARA LOUISE HARPER

EASY

Sizes
Child's average
Woman's average

Finished Felted Measurements
Circumference: Approx 22 inches for Child and 23 inches for Woman
Depth: Approx 6½ inches for Child and 8½ inches for Woman
Measurements achieved using yarn and color specified; results may vary depending on yarn, yarn color and felting time.

Materials
- Plymouth Galway Worsted 100 percent medium weight wool (210 yds/100g per skein): 1 skein each yellow #88 (MC for child's, CC for adult's), teal #139 (CC for child's, MC for adult's) and aqua #116
- Size 11 (8mm) circular and double-pointed needles or size needed to obtain gauge
- Stitch markers
- Tapestry needle

Pre-Felted Gauge
15 sts and 16 rows = 4 inches/10cm in St st
Exact gauge is not critical; make sure your sts are loose and airy.

Special Abbreviation
Dec2 (Decrease 2): Sl 2 sts as if to k2tog, k1, p2sso.

Pattern Note
Change to dpn when sts no longer fit comfortably on circular needle.

Child's Cloche
With MC, cast on 98 sts.
Join without twisting; place marker between first and last sts.
Knit 5 rnds.
Colorwork Rnds 1 and 2: *K1 with MC, k1 with CC; rep from * around.

With MC, knit 3 rnds.
Dec rnd: Dec 6 sts evenly around. (92 sts)
Knit 5 rnds.
Rep Colorwork Rnds 1 and 2.
Inc rnd: Using MC, knit and inc 8 sts evenly around. (100 sts)
*Knit 3 rnds.
Inc rnd: Inc 10 sts evenly around. (110 sts)
Rep from * (120 sts).
Knit 6 rnds.

Rep Colorwork Rnds 1 and 2.
With MC, knit 1 rnd.
Inc rnd 1: Inc 8 sts evenly around.
  (104 sts)
Knit 3 rnds.
Inc rnd 2: Inc 10 sts evenly around.
  (114 sts)
Knit 3 rnds.
Inc rnd 3: Inc 6 sts evenly around.
  (120 sts)
Knit 6 rnds.

Crown
Work as for child's cloche.

Felting
Follow basic felting instructions
  on page 168 until hat is just
  slightly smaller than finished
  measurements or desired size.
Block by stretching over a bowl that
  is just slightly larger than desired
  head size, or a hat form.

Pompom
Cut two cardboard circles 3 inches
  in diameter. Cut a hole in the
  center of each circle, about ½ inch
  in diameter. Thread a tapestry
  needle with a length of aqua yarn
  doubled. Holding both circles
  together, insert needle through
  center hole, over the outside edge,
  and through center again until
  entire circle is covered and the
  center hole is filled (thread more
  length of yarn as needed).
With sharp scissors, cut yarn between
  the two circles all around the
  circumference.
Using two 12-inch strands of yarn,
  slip yarn between circles and
  overlap yarn ends 2 or 3 times to
  prevent knot from slipping, pull
  tightly and tie into a firm knot.
  Remove cardboard and fluff out
  pompom by rolling it between
  your hands. Trim even with
  scissors, leaving tying ends for
  attaching pompom to hat. Attach
  to top of hat. ✱

Crown
Dec rnd 1: *K7, Dec2; rep from *
  around. (96 sts)
Knit 2 rnds.
Dec rnd 2: *K5, Dec2; rep from *
  around. (72 sts)
Knit 2 rnds.
Dec rnd 3: *K3, Dec2; rep from *
  around. (48 sts)
Knit 2 rnds.
Dec rnd 4: *K1, Dec2; rep from *
  around. (24 sts)
Next 2 rnds: K2tog around. (6 sts)
Thread yarn through rem sts, pull

tight and secure.
Weave in all ends.

Adult's Cloche
With MC, cast on 102 sts.
Join without twisting; place marker
  between first and last sts.
Knit 12 rnds.
Colorwork Rnds 1 and 2: *K1 with
  MC, k1 with CC; rep from * around.
Using CC, knit 5 rnds.
Dec rnd: Dec 6 sts evenly around.
  (96 sts)
Knit 10 rnds.

Smooth & Furry Hat & Scarf

PAIR THIS HAT WITH ITS COORDINATING SCARF AND YOU'RE READY FOR A NIGHT OUT, NO MATTER HOW COLD IT MAY BE.

DESIGNS BY SCARLET TAYLOR

EASY

For matching mittens, see page 39.

HAT

Size
Woman's average

Finished Felted Measurement
Circumference: 21½ inches
Measurements achieved using yarn and color specified; results may vary depending on yarn, yarn color and felting time.

Materials

- Plymouth Galway 100 percent wool medium weight yarn (210 yds/100g per ball): 1 ball red #16 (A)
- Plymouth Firenze 30 percent wool/30 percent acrylic/40 percent nylon bulky weight yarn (55 yds/50g per ball): 1 ball rose #430 (B)
- Size 11 (8mm) double-pointed and 16-inch circular needles or size needed to obtain gauge
- Stitch markers (1 in contrasting color for beg of rnd)
- Tapestry needle

Pre-Felted Gauge
14 sts and 18 rnds = 4 inches/10cm in St st with 1 strand A
12 sts and 16 rnds = 4 inches/10cm in St st with 1 strand each A and B held tog
Exact gauge is not critical; make sure your sts are loose and airy.

Special Abbreviation
M1 (Make 1): Insert tip of LH needle under horizontal strand between st just worked and next st and k1-tbl.

Pattern Notes
One strand each of A and B are held tog for brim.
Change to dpn when sts no longer fit comfortably on circular needle.

Hat
Brim
With circular needle and 1 strand each of A and B held tog, cast on 75 sts.
Join without twisting; place marker between first and last sts.
Purl 2 rnds.
Knit 11 rnds. Cut B
Next rnd: With A, k3, M1, [k7, M1] 10

times, k2. (86 sts)

Work even in St st until hat measures approx 11½ inches from end of brim.

Crown
Next rnd: K22, place marker, [k21, place marker] 2 times, k22.

Next rnd: Knit.

Next rnd: *K1, ssk, knit to 2 sts before marker, k2tog, sl marker; rep from * to end of rnd. (78 sts)

Rep last 2 rnds until 14 sts rem.

Next rnd: Knit.

Next rnd: K2tog around. (7 sts)

Next rnd: Knit.

Next rnd: K2tog, k3tog, k2tog. (3 sts)

Sl all 3 sts to 1 dpn.

I-Cord Trim
Next row: *K3, do not turn; sl sts back to LH needle; rep from * for approx 3 inches.

Bind off.

Weave in all ends.

Felting
Follow basic felting instructions on page 168 until hat is just slightly smaller than finished measurements or desired size.

Block by stretching over a bowl that is just slightly larger than desired head size, or a hat form.

SCARF

Finished Felted Measurements
Approx 5½ x 76 inches

Measurements achieved using yarn and color specified; results may vary depending on yarn, yarn color and felting time.

Materials
- Plymouth Galway Worsted 100 percent wool medium weight yarn (210 yds/100g per ball): 3 balls red #16 (A)

- Plymouth Firenze 30 percent wool/30 percent acrylic/40 percent nylon bulky weight yarn (55 yds/50g per ball): 3 balls rose #430 (B)
- Size 11 (8mm) straight needles or size needed to obtain gauge
- Tapestry needle

Pre-Felted Gauge
13 sts and 16 rows = 4 inches/10cm in St st with 2 strands held tog

Exact gauge is not critical; make sure your sts are loose and airy.

Stripe Pattern
Rows 1–22: With 2 strands of A held tog, work in St st.

Rows 23–44: With 1 strand each of A and B held tog, work in St st.

Rep Rows 1–44 for Stripe pattern.

Pattern Note
This scarf is worked throughout with either 2 strands A, or 1 strand each A and B held tog, as instructed.

Scarf
With 2 strands A held tog, cast on 21 sts. Knit 3 rows.

Next row (WS): K3, purl to last 3 sts, k3.

Maintaining first and last 3 sts in garter st for borders, [work Stripe pat] 8 times; work Rows 1–22.

Knit 4 rows.

Weave in all yarn ends.

Felting
Follow basic felting instructions on page 168 until finished measurements are obtained or scarf is desired size ✳

Snowflakes Scarf & Headband

IT'S WINTER AND THERE ARE SNOWFLAKES, SNOWFLAKES EVERYWHERE—WHY NOT AROUND YOUR NECK?

DESIGNS BY SCARLET TAYLOR

INTERMEDIATE

For matching mittens, see page 41.

SCARF

Finished Felted Measurements

Approx 5½ x 58 inches, excluding fringe

Measurements achieved using yarn and colors specified; results may vary depending on yarn, yarn color and felting time.

Materials

- Plymouth Suri Merino 55 percent suri alpaca/45 percent extra-fine merino medium weight yarn (109 yds/50g per ball): 3 balls white #100 (A), 2 balls light blue #2174 (B)
- Size 5 (3.25mm) double-pointed needles
- Size 7 (4.5mm) straight needles
- Size 9 (5.5mm) straight needles or size needed to obtain gauge
- Stitch holder
- Stitch markers
- Tapestry needle
- Sharp sewing needle small enough to pass through beads
- White sewing thread
- 77 crystal AB bicone beads*

*Sample made with Crystal Innovations beads from Pure Allure Inc.

Pre-Felted Gauge

18 sts and 21 rows = 4 inches/10cm in St st with larger straight needles

Exact gauge is not critical; make sure your sts are loose and airy.

Pattern Notes

The colorwork of this scarf is worked using a combination of intarsia and Fair Isle methods.

Sl markers as you come to them.

Scarf

With smaller straight needles and B, cast on 39 sts.

Work in garter st for 3 rows.

Change to larger needles, and beg working in St st between 3-st garter borders in B.

Set-up row (RS): K3 B for garter st border, join A and k9 A, place marker, join a 2nd ball of B and work Row 1 of Snowflakes Chart on page 33 over 15 sts, place marker, k9 A, join 3rd ball of B and k3 B for garter-st border.

CONTINUED ON PAGE 32

Rolled Brim Hat

THE WHIMSICAL FURRY I-CORD TRIM LENDS THIS BEAUTIFUL, YET SIMPLE, ROLLED BRIM HAT AN AIR OF PANACHE!

DESIGN BY NAZANIN S. FARD

EASY

Size
Woman's average

Finished Felted Measurement
Circumference: 22 inches
Measurement achieved using yarn and color specified; results may vary depending on yarn, yarn color and felting time.

Materials
- Plymouth Galway Worsted 100 percent wool medium weight yarn (210 yds/100g per ball): 2 balls lavender #89 (A) **[4 MEDIUM]**
- Plymouth Firenze 30 percent wool/30 percent acrylic/40 percent nylon bulky weight yarn (55 yds/50g per ball): 1 ball gold #435 (B) **[5 BULKY]**
- Plymouth Combolo 66 percent nylon/30 percent tactel/4 percent polyester bulky weight yarn (47 yds/50g per ball): 1 ball terra cotta #1027 (C)
- Size 10½ (6.5mm) double-pointed and 16-inch circular needles or size needed to obtain gauge
- Stitch markers
- Tapestry needle

Pre-Felted Gauge
14 sts and 20 rnds = 4 inches/10cm in St st with A
Exact gauge is not critical; make sure your sts are loose and airy.

Pattern Note
Change to dpns when sts no longer fit comfortably on circular needle.

Hat
Brim
With circular needle and A, cast on 120 sts.
Join without twisting; place marker between first and last sts.
Work in St st for 4 inches.

Crown
Dec rnd 1: *K2tog, k8; rep from * around. (108 sts)
Knit 2 rnds.
Dec rnd 2: *K2tog, k7; rep from * around. (96 sts)
Knit 2 rnds.
Dec rnd 3: *K2tog, k6; rep from * around. (84 sts)
Knit 1 rnd.
Dec rnd 4: *K2tog, k5; rep from * around. (72 sts)
Knit 1 rnd.
Dec rnd 5: K2tog around. (36 sts)
Next 3 rnds: Knit 1 rnd; [rep Dec rnd 5] twice. (9 sts)
Dec rnd 6: *K2tog; rep from * to last st, end k1. (5 sts)
Cut yarn, leaving a 6-inch tail.
Using tapestry needle, thread tail through rem sts, pull tight and secure.
Weave in all ends.

Felting
Follow basic felting instructions on page 168 until hat is just slightly smaller than finished measurements or desired size.
Block by stretching over a bowl that is just slightly larger than desired head size, or a hat form.

I-Cord Trim
With dpn, and B and C held tog, cast on 3 sts.
*K3, do not turn; sl sts back to LH needle; rep from * until I-cord measures 65 inches.
Bind off.
Weave in all ends.
Wrap the I-cord around the brim. Make a bow and let the ends hang. ✳

Touch of Fluff

A SOFT FLUFFY EDGE FRAMES THE FACE AND A FELTED CROWN WARMS THE HEAD—PERFECT!

DESIGN BY NAZANIN S. FARD

EASY

Size
Woman's average

Finished Felted Measurement
Circumference: 22 inches
Measurement achieved using yarn and color specified; results may vary depending on yarn, yarn color and felting time.

Materials
- Plymouth Galway Worsted 100 percent wool medium weight yarn (210 yds/100g per ball): 1 ball olive #59 (A)
- Plymouth Firenze 30 percent wool/30 percent acrylic/40 percent nylon bulky weight yarn (55 yds/50g per ball): 1 ball teal #431 (B)
- Size 10½ (6.5mm) double-pointed and 24-inch circular needles or size needed to obtain gauge
- Stitch marker
- Tapestry needle

Pre-Felted Gauge
14 sts and 20 rows = 4 inches/10cm in St st with A
Exact gauge is not critical; make sure your sts are loose and airy.

Pattern Stitch
Garter st in-the-round
Knit 1 rnd, purl 1 rnd.
Rep these 2 rnds for pat.

Pattern Note
Change to dpn when sts no longer fit comfortably on circular needle.

Hat
Brim
With A, cast on 100 sts. Join without twisting; place marker between first and last sts.
With A and B held tog, work 14 rnds of garter st.
Cut B.

Sides
Dec rnd: With A, *k2tog, k8; rep from * around. (90 sts)
Work 7 inches in St st.

Crown
Dec rnd 1: K2tog around. (45 sts)
Knit 1 rnd.

Dec rnd 2: *K2tog, k1; rep from * around. (30 sts)
Knit 1 rnd.
Dec rnd 3: Rep Dec rnd 1. (15 sts)
Knit 1 rnd.
Dec rnd 4: K3tog around. (5 sts)
Cut A, leaving a 6-inch tail.
Using tapestry needle, thread tail through rem sts, pull tight and secure.
Weave in all ends.

Felting
Follow basic felting instructions on page 168 until hat is just slightly smaller than finished measurements or desired size.
Block by stretching over a bowl that is just slightly larger than desired head size, or a hat form. ✻

Fun With Fiber

COMBINE WOOL AND A GLITZY NOVELTY YARN FOR A TWEEDY LOOK THAT SEEMS LIKE MAGIC.

DESIGN BY LAURA ANDERSSON

EASY

Size
Woman's average

Finished Felted Measurement
Circumference: Approx 22 inches
Measurement achieved using yarn and colors specified; results may vary depending on yarn, yarn color and felting time.

Materials
- Plymouth Eros Glitz 86 percent nylon/10 percent rayon/4 percent lurex medium weight yarn (158 yds/50g per ball): 2 balls citrus #188 (MC)
- Plymouth Galway Worsted 100 percent wool medium weight yarn (210 yds/100g per ball): 1 ball each beige #138 (A), orange #91 (B), and lime #127 (C).
- Size 11 (8mm) double-pointed and 16-inch circular needles or size needed to obtain gauge
- Stitch markers (1 in contrasting color to mark beg of rnd)
- Tapestry needle

Pre-Felted Gauge
14 sts and 20 rows = 4 inches/10cm in St st with 2 strands held tog
Exact gauge is not critical; make sure your sts are loose and airy.

Pattern Notes
One strand each of MC and A, B, or C are held tog throughout.

Change to dpns when sts no longer fit comfortably on circular needle.

Hat
With circular needle and MC and A held tog, cast on 84 sts.
Join without twisting; place marker between first and last sts.
Knit 7 rnds.
Work k5, p1 rib until hat measures 3¼ inches from beg.
Cut A.

Orange Stripe
Join B and continue k5, p1 rib for 2¾ inches.
Cut B.

Green Stripe
Join C and continue k5, p1 rib until hat measures 10½ inches from beg.

Crown
Set up rnd: *K2tog, k3, p1, place marker; rep from * around. (70 sts)

Next rnd: Knit the k sts and purl the p sts.

Dec rnd: *K2tog, work in rib as established to marker; rep from * around.

Rep last 2 rnds until 14 sts rem.

K2tog around until 3 sts rem.

Sl all 3 sts to 1 dpn.

I-Cord Trim

Next 5 rows: *K3, do not turn; sl sts back to LH needle; rep from *.

Cut yarn, leaving a 5-inch tail.

Using tapestry needle, thread tail through rem sts, and pull tight; bury tail in center of I-cord.

Weave in all ends.

Felting

Felt lightly either by hand or machine, following the basic felting instructions on page 168 until hat is just slightly smaller than finished measurements or desired size.

Block by stretching over a bowl that is just slightly larger than desired head size, or a hat form. ✱

Wrapped With Color Scarf

SIMPLE INTARSIA BRINGS THIS COLOR-BLOCKED SCARF TO LIFE. WEAR THIS SKINNY CREATION INSIDE OR OUT.

DESIGN BY SARA LOUISE HARPER

EASY

Finished Felted Measurements

Approx 3½ x 72 inches, excluding fringe

Measurements achieved using yarn and colors specified; results may vary depending on yarn, yarn color and felting time.

Materials

- Plymouth Galway Worsted 100 percent wool medium weight yarn (210 yds/100g per ball): 1 ball each mulberry #141 (A), pink #114 (B), aqua #116 (C), teal #139 (D) and yellow #88 (E)
- Size 11 (8 mm) straight needles or size needed to obtain gauge
- Tapestry needle

Pre-Felted Gauge

15 sts and 16 rows = 4 inches/10cm in St st

Exact gauge is not critical; make sure your sts are loose and airy.

Pattern Notes

The Chart is worked using the intarsia method using separate lengths of yarn for each color. When switching from one color to the next, bring new yarn up from under previous yarn to lock sts and prevent holes.

Each row of Chart is worked twice: Knit 1 row, purl 1 row.

Scarf

With A, cast on 20 sts.

Purl 1 row.
Work Chart twice (see Pattern Notes).
Work Rows 1–34.
With A, knit 1 row.
Bind off.
Weave in all ends in like-color areas.

Felting

Follow basic felting instructions on page 168 until finished measurements are obtained or scarf is desired size.

Shape if necessary (scarf can be stretched slightly to elongate) and allow to dry thoroughly.

Fringe

Cut 28 (18-inch) strands of A. *Fold one strand in half and thread through a tapestry needle. With RS facing and beg at corner of one narrow edge, insert needle through fabric from RS to WS. Remove yarn from needle and pull loose ends through folded section. Draw knot up firmly. Rep from *, placing 14 evenly spaced fringes along each narrow end. Trim even to 8 inches or desired length. ✻

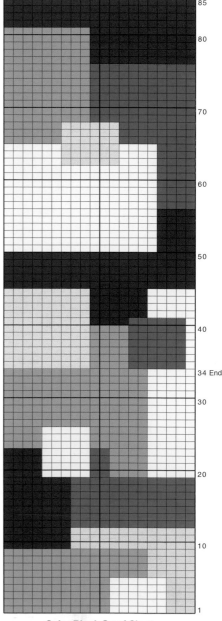

COLOR KEY
- ■ Mulberry (A)
- ☐ Pink (B)
- ■ Aqua (C)
- ■ Teal (D)
- ☐ Yellow (E)

Color Block Scarf Chart

Note: Work entire scarf in St st and work a knit row and a purl row for each row on pattern chart.

Added Glitz Scarf

THIS EASY SCARF IS KNIT LENGTHWISE WITH LUXURIOUS NOVELTY AND MOHAIR YARNS, THEN LIGHTLY FELTED.

DESIGN BY CHRISTINE L. WALTER

BEGINNER

Finished Felted Measurements

Approx 7 x 70 inches, excluding fringe
Measurements achieved using yarns and colors specified; results may vary depending on yarn, yarn color and felting time.

Materials

- Plymouth Odyssey Glitz 60 percent nylon/37 percent wool/3 percent lamé bulky weight yarn (66 yds/50g per ball): 3 balls gray #921 (A) **[5 BULKY]**
- Plymouth Outback Mohair 70 percent mohair/26 percent wool/4 percent nylon bulky weight yarn (218 yds/100g per skein): 1 skein gray #865 (B)
- Plymouth Eros Extreme 100 percent nylon super bulky weight yarn (98 yds/100g per skein): 1 skein silver #117 (C) **[6 SUPER BULKY]**

  or

  Plymouth Eros 100 percent nylon medium weight yarn (165 yds/50g per ball): 1 ball silver #117 (C)
- Plymouth Jungle 100 percent nylon super bulky weight yarn (61 yds/50g per ball) 1 ball earth #117 (D)
- Size 17 (12.75 mm) straight needles or size needed to obtain gauge
- Size I/9 (5.5mm) crochet hook

Pre-Felted Gauge

8 sts and 12 rows = 4 inches/10cm in garter st with A and B held tog.

Exact gauge is not critical; make sure your sts are loose and airy.

Pattern Notes

One strand each of A and B are held tog throughout.

The scarf is very loosely knit on a large needle, and the sts have a tendency to flatten out in felting; this will result in a longer scarf.

Photographed model uses Eros Extreme (C) for fringe. If using thinner Eros for fringe, use it double or triple.

Scarf

With 1 strand each of A and B held tog, cast on 128 sts.
Knit 22 rows.
Bind off loosely.
Cut yarn.
Weave in ends.

Felting

Lightly felt scarf either by hand or machine, following basic felting instructions on page 168, until finished measurements are obtained or scarf is desired size. Be careful not to overfelt.
Block scarf lightly by laying it flat and pinning to measurements. Allow to dry thoroughly.

Fringe

Cut 22 (12-inch) strands each of C and D. *Fold one strand in half. With RS facing and beg at corner of one edge, use crochet hook to draw folded end from RS to WS. Pull loose ends through folded section. Draw knot up firmly. Rep from *, placing 11 evenly spaced fringes along each short edge, alternating C and D. Trim even. ✷

Covered in Stripes

FELTING NOVELTY YARN AND BABY ALPACA PUTS A SPARKLY, DRAPEY SPIN ON THIS SIMPLE GARTER STITCH SCARF.

DESIGN BY CINDY ADAMS

BEGINNER

Finished Felted Measurements

Approx 9½ x 63 inches

Measurements achieved using yarn and color specified; results may vary depending on yarn, yarn color and felting time.

Materials

- Plymouth Baby Alpaca DK 100 percent baby alpaca light weight yarn (125 yds/50g per ball): 2 balls wine #2020 (A)
- Plymouth Combolo 66 percent nylon/30 percent tactel/4 percent polyester bulky weight yarn (47 yds/50g per ball): 3 balls wine #1038 (B)
- Size 11 (8mm) straight needles or size needed to obtain gauge
- Tapestry needle

Pre-Felted Gauge

10 sts and 16 rows = 4 inches/10cm in garter st, alternating 2 rows A and 2 rows B

Exact gauge is not critical; make sure your sts are loose and airy.

Pattern Note

For all rows, sl first st wyif.

Scarf

With A, cast on 30 sts.

Knit 6 rows.

*Knit 2 rows with B.

Knit 2 rows with A.

Rep from * for 62 inches, ending with B.

Knit 6 rows with A.

Bind off.

Weave in ends.

Felting

Felt lightly, either by hand or by following basic felting instructions on page 168 until finished measurements are obtained or scarf is desired size. ✳

Fair Isle Hat continued from page 8

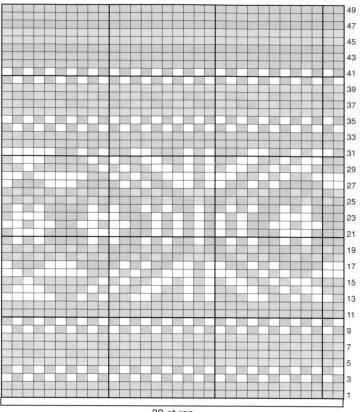

32-st rep

Fair Isle Chart

Felting

Follow basic felting instructions on page 168 until hat is just slightly smaller than finished measurements or desired size.

Block by stretching over a bowl that is just slightly larger than desired head size, or a hat form.

Finishing

When dry, pull the acrylic yarn at top of hat tight to close; tie a knot and secure the ends to WS. (The small hole will be covered with pompom.)

Pull the acrylic yarn around the edges of pompom to gather, then stuff center of pompom with leftover yarn or stuffing.

Pull acrylic yarn tight and secure.

Sew pompom to top of hat (to cover top opening). ✻

COLOR KEY	
▨	Tan (MC)
☐	White (A)
▨	Pink (B)
▨	Light green (C)

Snowflakes Scarf & Headband continued from page 19

Maintaining first and last 3 sts in B and garter st for borders throughout, continue in pat as established, rep Rows 1–26 of Snowflakes Chart between markers until scarf measures approx 70 inches from beg, ending with Row 26 of chart.

Change to B and smaller needles, and work 4 rows in garter st.

Sl sts onto holder.

I-Cord Fringe

With RS facing, sl first 3 sts from holder to dpn.

With B, work I-cord as follows: *K3, do not turn; sl sts back to LH needle; rep from * until cord is approx 4 inches long.

Bind off. Thread yarn through sts and fasten off, hiding end in center of I-cord.

Rep for each set of 3 sts across holder. (13 fringes)

With RS facing, smaller needles and B, pick up and knit 39 sts along cast-on edge.

Work I-cord fringe as for bind-off edge.

Weave in all ends.

Felting

Follow basic felting instructions on page 168 until finished measurements are obtained or scarf is desired size.

Finishing

When scarf is thoroughly dry, sew beads to snowflakes following Chart.

Sew on additional beads as desired in the outer white section.

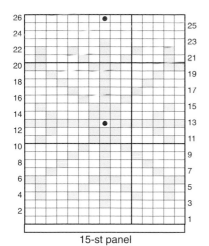

15-st panel

Snowflakes Scarf Chart

COLOR KEY
- ☐ White (A)
- ☐ Light blue (B)
- ⦿ Sew on bead after felting

HEADBAND

Size

Woman's average

Finished Felted Measurements

Circumference: Approx 21½ inches
Measurement achieved using yarn and color specified; results may vary depending on yarn, yarn color and felting time.

Materials

- Plymouth Suri Merino 55 percent suri alpaca/45 percent extra-fine merino medium weight yarn (109 yds/50g per ball): 1 ball each white #100 (A) and light blue #2174 (B)

- Size 7 (4.5mm) 16-inch circular knitting needle
- Size 9 (5.5mm) 16-inch circular knitting needle or size needed to obtain gauge
- Stitch marker
- Tapestry needle
- Sharp sewing needle small enough to pass through beads
- White sewing thread
- 36 crystal AB bicone beads*

*Sample made with Crystal Innovations beads from Pure Allure Inc.

Pre-Felted Gauge

18 sts and 21 rnds = 4 inches/10cm in stranded St st with larger needles
Exact gauge is not critical; make sure your sts are loose and airy.

Headband

With smaller needles and B, loosely cast on 108 sts. Join without twisting; place marker between first and last sts.

Border

Purl 1 rnd, knit 1 rnd, purl 1 rnd.

Color Pattern

Change to larger needles and St st.
Join A, and work 21 rnds of Snowflakes Chart.
Cut A.

Border

Change to smaller needles.
With B only, purl 1 rnd, knit 1 rnd, purl 1 rnd.
Bind off loosely.
Weave in all ends.

Felting

Follow basic felting instructions on page 168 until finished measurements are obtained or headband is desired size.

Finishing

When headband is thoroughly dry, sew beads to snowflakes, following Chart. ✳

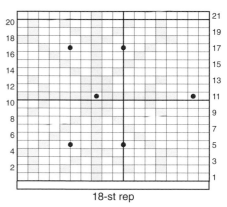

18-st rep

Snowflakes Headband Chart

COLOR KEY
- ☐ White (A)
- ☐ Light blue (B)
- ⦿ Sew on bead after felting

{ Warm Hands: Mittens & Wristers }

FELTED MITTENS KEEP HANDS
DRY AND WARM! WE'VE INCLUDED
INNOVATIVE STYLES FOR ALL AGES.

Ruffled-Cuff Mittens

MADE FROM SOFT AND CUDDLY ALPACA YARN, THESE MITTENS WILL KEEP LITTLE HANDS TOASTY.

DESIGN BY DONNA DRUCHUNAS

INTERMEDIATE

Sizes

Child's 4 (6, 8)
Instructions are given for smallest size with changes for larger sizes in parentheses. When only 1 number is given, it applies to all sizes.

Finished Felted Measurement

Wrist circumference: Approx 5½ (6, 7) inches
Measurements achieved using yarn and color specified; results may vary depending on yarn, yarn color and felting time.

Materials

- Plymouth Baby Alpaca Grande 100 percent baby alpaca bulky weight yarn (110 yds/100g per skein): 1 (2, 2) skeins wine/pink marl #2567
- Size 11 (8mm) double-pointed needles
- Size 15 (10mm) double-pointed needles or size needed to obtain gauge
- Stitch markers (1 in contrasting color for beg of rnd)
- Stitch holder
- Tapestry needle

Pre-Felted Gauge

8 sts and 11 rows = 4 inches/10cm over St st with larger needles
Exact gauge is not critical; make sure your sts are loose and airy.

Special Abbreviation

M1 (Make 1): Insert tip of LH needle under horizontal strand between st just worked and next st and k1-tbl.

Mitten

Cuff Ruffle

With larger needles, cast on 60 (72, 84) sts.
Distribute sts evenly on 3 or 4 dpns.
Join without twisting; place marker between first and last sts.
Rnds 1, 3 and 5: Knit.
Rnd 2: K2tog around. (30, 36, 42 sts)
Rnd 4: (K1, k2tog) around. (20, 24, 28 sts)

Rib

Change to smaller needles.
Work in k2, p2 rib for 1½ (2, 2½) inches.
Next rnd: Inc 6 sts evenly around. (26, 30, 34 sts)

Thumb Gusset

Change to larger needles and St st.
Set-up rnd: K1, place marker, p1, k1, p1, place marker, knit to end of rnd.
Work 2 rnds even.
Inc rnd: Knit to first marker, p1, M1, knit to 1 st before next marker, M1, p1, knit to end of rnd.
Rep Inc rnd every 3rd rnd until there

are 11 (13, 15) sts between markers. Work even until mitten measures 4 (4½, 5) inches from beg of rib.

Next rnd: Put the sts between the markers onto a holder; cast on 3 sts over the gap at the thumb; knit to end of rnd. (26, 30, 34 sts)

Hand

Work even until piece measures 6 (7, 8) inches from beg of rib.

Dec rnd: Dec 2 (0, 1) sts. (24, 30, 33 sts rem)

Shape Top

Distribute sts evenly on 3 needles.

Dec rnd: On each needle, k2tog, knit to last 2 sts, k2tog.

Rep Dec rnd every 3rd rnd 2 (3, 3) times. (6, 6, 9 sts)

Cut yarn, leaving a 6-inch tail.

Thread the tail through the rem sts; pull tight and secure.

Thumb

Sl the thumb sts from the holder to 2 dpns; with a 3rd dpn, pick up and knit 3 sts from the cast-on edge next to thumb. (14, 16, 18 sts)

Knit even for 1 (1½, 2) inches.

Dec rnd: K2tog around.

Cut yarn, leaving a 6-inch tail.

Thread tail through the rem sts; pull tight and secure.

Weave in ends.

Felting

Note: *This yarn is slow to begin felting, then shrinks very quickly.*

Follow basic felting instructions on page 168 until finished measurements are obtained or mittens are desired size. Dry flat, checking the felting every few minutes. ✳

Texture & Fluff Mittens

DRESS UP YOUR HANDS WHILE KEEPING THEM WARM IN THESE STRAWBERRY-RED MITTENS.

DESIGN BY SCARLET TAYLOR

EASY

For matching hat & scarf, see page 15.

Size
Woman's average

Finished Felted Measurement
Wrist circumference: Approx 8 inches
Measurement achieved using yarn and color specified; results may vary depending on yarn, yarn color and felting time.

Materials
- Plymouth Galway Worsted 100 percent wool medium weight yarn (210 yds/100g per ball): 1 ball red #16 (A)
- Plymouth Firenze 30 percent wool/30 percent acrylic/40 percent nylon bulky weight yarn (55 yds/50g per ball): 1 ball rose #430 (B)
- Size 7 (4.5mm) double-pointed needles
- Size 10½ (6.5mm) double-pointed needles
- Size 11 (8mm) straight needles or size needed to obtain gauge
- Small amount of worsted weight cotton yarn for waste-yarn edging
- Stitch holder
- Stitch markers
- Tapestry needle

Pre-Felted Gauge
14 sts and 18 rows = 4 inches/10cm in St st with largest needles and A
Exact gauge is not critical; make sure your sts are loose and airy.

Special Abbreviations
MB (Make Bobble): Knit into (front, back, front, back, then front again) of next st, making 5 sts in 1, turn. P5, turn. K2tog, k3tog; pass the k2tog st over last st and off needle. (1 st rem)

M1 (Make 1): Insert tip of LH needle under horizontal strand between st just worked and next st and k1-tbl.

Pattern Stitch
Bobble Pattern
Row 1 (RS): K11, MB, k1, MB, k4.
Rows 2 and all WS rows: Purl.
Row 3: K12, MB, k5.
Row 5: Knit.
Row 7: K4, MB, k1, MB, k11.
Row 9: K5, MB, k12.
Row 11: Knit.
Row 12: Purl.

Right Mitten: Work Rows 1–12 twice, then rep Rows 1–3 once more for pat.

Left Mitten: Work Rows 7-12, then work Rows 1-12, and 1-9 for pat.

Pattern Notes

For a smoother seam, sl first st of every row wyif. (This will not be repeated on every pat row.)

A temporary edging is added along the wrist edge with non-felting cotton yarn to stabilize the edge and to provide a "hole" in which to pick up sts for the un-felted cuff after the mitten is felted.

Right Mitten
Wrist

With straight needles and A, cast on 37 sts.

Slipping first st of every row (see Pattern Notes), work 8 rows in St st.

Thumb Gusset

Row 1 (RS): K18, place marker for thumb; M1, k1, M1; place marker for thumb, k18. (39 sts)

Row 2 and all WS rows: Purl.

Next row (RS): Beg with Row 1, work Bobble pat to marker, sl marker, M1, knit to next marker, M1, sl marker; knit to end.

Continue in pats as established, and rep last 2 rows until there are 15 sts between markers. (51 sts)

Hand

Row 1 (RS): Work Bobble pat to marker, place 15 thumb sts on holder, knit to end. (36 sts)

Work even in pats as established until mitten measures 7½ inches from beg, ending with a WS row and placing a marker between 2 center sts on last row.

Shape Top

Row 1 (RS): Sl 1, ssk, work in Bobble pat as established to 2 sts before marker, k2tog, sl marker; ssk, knit to last 3 sts, k2tog, k1. (32 sts)

Row 2: Purl.

[Rep Rows 1 and 2] twice, removing marker on last row. (24 sts)

Dec row: K2tog across. (12 sts)

Next row: Purl.

Rep last 2 rows, then work Dec row. (3 sts)

Cut yarn, leaving a 6-inch tail.

Thread tail through rem sts, pull tight and secure.

Thumb

With RS facing, return sts from holder to needle. Join yarn and work 8 rows even.

Next row (RS): K2tog across, end k1. (8 sts)

Next row and all WS rows: Purl.

Next 2 RS rows: K2tog across. (2 sts)

Cut yarn, leaving a 6-inch tail.

Thread tail through rem sts, pull tight and secure.

Wrist Waste-Yarn Edging

With cotton yarn, pick up and knit 30 sts along cast-on edge.

Knit 2 rows.

Bind off.

Sew side and thumb seams.

If necessary, duplicate st over hole where thumb and mitten divide.

Weave in yarn ends.

Left Mitten

Work same as for Right Mitten to beg of thumb incs.

Thumb Gusset

Row 1 (RS): K18; place marker for thumb; M1, k1, M1; place marker for thumb, k18. (39 sts)

Row 2 and all WS rows: Purl.

Next row (RS): Knit to first thumb marker, sl marker, M1, knit to 2nd marker, M1, sl marker; beg with Row 7, work Bobble pat to end.

Continuing in pats as established, rep last 2 rows for thumb incs until there are 15 sts between markers. (51 sts)

Hand

Row 1 (RS): Knit to first marker, place 15 thumb sts on st holder, work in Bobble pat as established to end. (36 sts).

Work even until mitten measures approx 7½ inches from beg, ending with a WS row and placing a marker between 2 center sts on last row.

Work top and thumb as for right mitten.

Work wrist waste-yarn edging and sew seams as for right mitten.

Weave in all ends.

Felting

Follow basic felting instructions on page 168 until finished measurements are obtained or mittens are desired size.

Finishing
Cuff

Allow mitten to dry completely.

With smaller double-pointed needles and A, pick up and knit 30 sts around mitten wrist edge, through the center of "hole" kept open by each cotton st.

Place marker and join.

Work in k1, p1 rib for 2 inches.

Change to larger dpns and B, and work in garter st (knit 1 rnd, purl 1 rnd) for 2¼ inches.

Bind off loosely.

Fold fur cuff over ribbing and tack in place. ✳

Snowflakes Mittens

BE A KID AGAIN—BUILD A SNOWMAN WEARING THESE WARM MITTENS AND YOU WON'T WORRY ABOUT FROSTBITE.

DESIGN BY SCARLET TAYLOR

INTERMEDIATE

For matching scarf & headband, see page 19.

Size
Woman's average

Finished Felted Measurement
Wrist circumference: Approx 8 inches
Measurement achieved using yarn and color specified; results may vary depending on yarn, yarn color and felting time.

Materials
- Plymouth Suri Merino 55 percent suri alpaca/45 percent extra-fine merino wool medium weight yarn (109 yds/50g per ball): 2 balls light blue #2174 (A) and 1 ball white #100 (B)

  4 MEDIUM
- Size 9 (5.5mm) straight needles or size needed to obtain gauge
- Stitch holder
- Stitch markers
- Tapestry needle
- Sharp sewing needle small enough to pass through beads
- White sewing thread
- 36 crystal AB bicone beads*

*Sample made with Crystal Innovations beads from Pure Allure Inc.

Pre-Felted Gauge
18 sts and 21 rows = 4 inches/10cm in St st
Exact gauge is not critical; make sure your sts are loose and airy.

Special Abbreviations
M1 (Make 1): Insert tip of LH needle under horizontal strand between st just worked and next st and k1-tbl.
Pm (place marker): Place marker on needle.

Pattern Note
For a smoother seam, sl first st of every row wyif. (This will not be repeated on every pattern row.)

Right Mitten
Cuff
With A, cast on 41 sts.
Row 1 (RS): Sl 1 wyif, *p2, k2; rep from * across row.
Slipping the first st of every row (see Pattern Note), continue in k2, p2 rib as established for approx 3½ inches, ending with a WS row.
Work 8 rows in St st.

Thumb Gusset

Row 1 (RS): K20, pm for thumb; M1, k1, M1; pm for thumb; k20. (43 sts)

Row 2 and all WS rows: Purl.

Rep Rows 1 and 2 until there are 15 sts between markers and *at the same time*, when mitten measures 2 inches above rib, set up snowflakes pat as follows:

Next row (RS): K2, M1, k2, pm, work Row 1 of snowflakes pat (see Chart) over next 11 sts, pm, continue in pat as established to end row. (56 sts)

Hand

Row 1 (RS): Work in pat as established to thumb marker, place the 15 thumb sts onto st holder, knit to end of row. (41 sts)

Work even until piece measures approx 8 inches above rib, ending with a RS row.

Next row: Work 20 sts in pat, pm for center, purl to last 3 sts, p2tog, p1. (40 sts)

Shape Top

Row 1 (RS): *Sl 1, ssk, work in pat to 2 sts before center marker, k2tog, sl marker, ssk, knit to last 3 sts, k2tog, k1. (36 sts)

Row 2: Work even in pat.

[Rep Rows 1 and 2] twice, removing marker on last row. (28 sts)

Next row: K2tog across. (14 sts)

Next row: Purl.

Next row: K2tog across. (7 sts)

Next row: Purl.

Next row: K2tog, k3tog, k2tog (3 sts)

Next row: Purl.

Cut yarn, leaving a 6-inch tail.

Thread yarn through rem sts; pull tight and secure.

Thumb

With RS facing, return sts from holder to needle.

Join yarn and work 16 rows even in St st.

Next row: K2tog across, end k1. (8 sts)

Next row and every WS row: Purl.

Next 2 RS rows: K2tog across. (2 sts)

Cut yarn, leaving a 6-inch tail.

Thread through rem sts, pull tight and secure.

Sew side, cuff and thumb seams.

If necessary, duplicate st over hole where thumb and mitten divide.

Weave in all ends.

Left Mitten

Work as for right mitten to thumb gusset, remembering to sl the first st of every row.

Thumb Gusset

Row 1 (RS): K20; pm for thumb; M1, k1, M1; pm for thumb; k20. (43 sts)

Row 2 and all WS rows: Work even in pat.

Rep Rows 1 and 2 until there are 15 sts between markers and *at the same time*, when mitten measures 2 inches above rib, set up snowflakes pat as follows:

Next row (RS): K20, continue to inc for thumb, k5, pm, work Row 1 of snowflakes pat (see Chart) over next 11 sts, pm, k2, M1, k2. (56 sts)

Hand

Row 1 (RS): K20, place the 15 thumbs sts onto st holder, continue in snowflake pat as established over rem 21 sts. (41 sts)

Work even in pat established until mitten measures approx 8 inches above rib, ending with a RS row.

Next row: Sl 1, p2tog, p18, pm, work in pat to end. (40 sts)

Work top and thumb as for right mitten.

Sew seams as for right mitten.

Weave in all ends.

Felting

Follow basic felting instructions on page 168 until finished measurements are obtained or mittens are desired size.

Finishing

When mittens are thoroughly dry, sew beads to snowflakes, following Chart. ✳

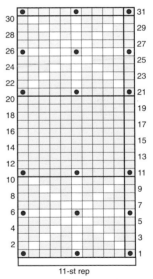

Snowflakes Mittens Chart

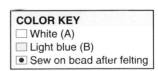

COLOR KEY
☐ White (A)
☐ Light blue (B)
⊡ Sew on bead after felting

Keep-Out-the-Cold Mittens

GOING SLEDDING? DON'T WORRY ABOUT GETTING COLD, WET HANDS WHEN WEARING THESE HARDY MITTENS.

DESIGN BY DONNA DRUCHUNAS

INTERMEDIATE

Sizes

Adult's medium (large)
Instructions are given for smaller size, with larger size in parentheses. When only 1 number is given, it applies to all sizes.

Finished Felted Measurement

Wrist circumference: Approx 8 (9) inches
Measurement achieved using yarns and colors specified; results may vary depending on yarn, yarn color and felting time.

Materials

- Plymouth Outback Wool 100 percent wool medium weight yarn (370 yds/200g per skein): 1 skein plum variegated #958 (A), *or* Plymouth Galway Worsted 100 percent wool medium weight yarn (210 yds/100g per ball): 2 skeins hot pink #135 (A)
- Plymouth Outback Mohair 70 percent mohair, 26 percent wool, 4 percent nylon bulky weight yarn (218 yds/100g per skein): 1 skein blue/purple multi #858 (B)
- Size 15 (10mm) double-pointed needles or size needed to obtain gauge
- Dog brush or hairbrush with metal bristles
- Tapestry needle

- Stitch markers
- Stitch holder
- Size G/6 (4.25 mm) crochet hook (optional)

Pre-Felted Gauge

9 sts and 12 rows = 4 inches/10cm in St st holding 2 strands tog
Exact gauge is not critical; make sure your sts are loose and airy.

Special Abbreviation

M1 (Make 1): Insert tip of LH needle under horizontal strand between st just worked and next st and k1-tbl.

Pattern Notes

You have the option of using 1 of 2 wool yarns for this project. Both are medium-weight yarns, but Outback Wool is a bit heavier than Galway Worsted. Using it will result in a denser mitten after felting.

Work with 1 strand each of A and B or with 2 strands of A held tog as instructed.

Sl markers when you come to them.

Mittens

Cuff

With A and B held tog, cast on 24 (28) sts.

Distribute on 3 dpn and join without twisting; place marker between first and last sts.

Work in k2, p2 rib until cuff measures 3 inches.

Cut B and add another strand of A.

Next rnd: Change to St st, and inc 2 sts evenly around. (26, 30 sts)

Thumb Gusset

Set up rnd: K1, place marker, p1, k1, p1, place marker, knit to end of rnd.

Work 2 rnds even.

Inc rnd: Knit to marker, sl marker, p1, M1, knit to next marker, M1, p1, sl marker, knit to end of rnd.

Rep Inc rnd every 3rd rnd until there are 11 (13) sts between markers.

Work 4 rnds even.

Next rnd: Knit to marker, put all sts between markers onto a holder; cast on 3 sts over the gap at the thumb and rejoin; knit to end of rnd. (26, 30 sts)

Hand

Work even in St st for 18 rnds.

Next rnd: Dec 2 (0) sts evenly. (24, 30 sts rem)

Shape Top

Distribute sts evenly on 3 dpns, 8 (10) sts on each needle.

Dec rnd: On each needle, k2tog, knit to last 2 sts on needle, k2tog. (18, 24 sts rem)

[Rep Dec rnd every 3rd rnd] 2 (3) times. (6 sts rem)

Cut yarn, leaving a 6-inch tail.

Thread the tail through the rem sts; pull tight and secure.

Thumb

Sl the thumb sts from the holder onto 2 dpns.

Pick up 3 sts from the cast-on edge next to thumb. (14, 16 sts)

Knit 10 (12) rnds even.

Dec rnd: K2tog around. (7, 8 sts rem)

Cut yarn leaving a 6-inch tail.

Thread the tail through the rem sts, pull tight and secure.

Weave in ends.

Felting

Follow basic felting instructions on page 168 until finished measurements are obtained or mittens are desired size.

Check the felting every few minutes. The Outback Wool yarn felts slowly, so you may need to run it through 2 or 3 agitation cycles to get it to shrink enough. The Galway Worsted yarn felts quickly, so keep a close eye on the mittens during felting to ensure that they don't shrink too much.

When mittens are thoroughly dry, brush the mohair cuffs with a dog brush or a hairbrush with metal bristles to fluff up the fiber.

Crochet Trim (optional)

Using a single strand of mohair, work 3 rows of single crochet around the cuff. If you have trouble pushing the crochet hook through the felted cuff, use the tapestry needle to poke holes about ¼ inch apart around the entire cuff, then make the crochet sts in these locations.

Fasten off.

Weave in ends. ✽

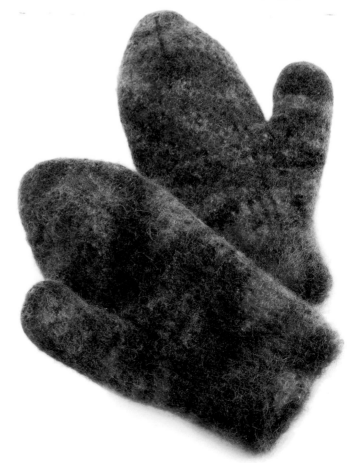

Checks & Stripes Mittens

TRY THESE EASY-TO-KNIT MITTENS THE NEXT TIME YOU WANT TO ADD A LITTLE SPLASH TO YOUR WINTER WARDROBE.

DESIGN BY SARA LOUISE HARPER

EASY

Sizes

Child's small (child's large, adult's small, adult's large) Instructions are given for smallest size, with larger sizes in parentheses. When only 1 number is given, it applies to all sizes.

Finished Felted Measurements

Wrist circumference: Approx 6¾ (7½, 8, 8¾) inches

Measurement achieved using yarn and colors specified; results may vary depending on yarn, yarn color and felting time.

Materials

- Plymouth Galway Worsted 100 percent wool medium weight yarn (210 yds/100g per ball):

    Child's: 1 skein each of teal #139 (A), aqua #116 (B) and pink #135 (C)

    Adult's: 1 skein each of charcoal #134 (A), black #9 (B) and mint #111 (C)
- Size 11 (8mm) straight needles or size needed to obtain gauge
- Stitch holder
- Stitch markers
- Tapestry needle

Pre-Felted Gauge

15 sts and 16 rows = 4 inches/10cm in St st

Exact gauge is not critical; make sure your sts are loose and airy.

Special Abbreviation

M1 (Make 1): Insert tip of LH needle under horizontal strand between st just worked and next st and k1-tbl.

Stitch Patterns

A. Checks (multiple of 2 sts)

Rows 1 and 3 (RS): *K2 C, k2 B; rep from * across, ending either k2 C or k2 B.

Row 2 and all WS rows: Purl colors in order established.

Rows 5 and 7: *K2 B, k2 C; rep from * across, ending either k2 B or k2 C.

Rows 9–12: Work as for Rows 1–4.

B. Stripes

Rows 1–4: With B, work in St st.

Rows 5–8: With A, work in St st.

Rep Rows 1–8 for Stripes pat.

Pattern Notes

Left and right mittens are worked the same.

For a smoother seam, sl first st of every row wyif. (This will not be repeated on every row.)

Mitten

Cuff

With B, cast on 30 (34, 36, 40) sts.

Working 2 rows in St st, remembering to sl the first st of each row.

Next row (RS): Inc 4 sts evenly across. (34, 38, 40, 44 sts)

Work 5 rows even in St st.

Join C and work 12 rows of Checks pat.

Beg Stripes pat, and work 2 rows.

Next row (RS): Inc 6 sts evenly across. (40, 44, 46, 50 sts)

Work 1 row even.

Thumb Gusset

Row 1 (RS): K19 (21, 22, 24), place marker, M1, k2, M1, place marker, k19 (21, 22, 24). (42, 46, 48, 52 sts)

Row 2 and all WS rows: Purl.

Row 3: Knit to marker, sl marker, M1, knit to next marker, M1, sl marker, knit to end.

Rep Rows 2 and 3 until there are 12 (14, 16, 16) sts between markers, ending with Row 2. (50, 56, 60, 64 sts)

Next row (RS): Knit to marker, place thumb sts on holder, knit to end. (40, 44, 46, 50 sts)

Hand

Continue Stripe pat and work even for 21 (25, 27, 33) rows, ending with a WS row.

Shape Top

Row 1 (RS): K0 (0, 2, 2), *k2tog, k2; rep from * to end of row. (30, 33, 35, 38 sts)

Row 2 and WS rows: Purl.

Row 3: K2tog 0 (0, 1, 1) time(s); *k1, k2tog; rep from * to end of row. (20, 22, 23, 25 sts)

Row 5: K2tog across row, end k0 (0, 1, 1). (10, 11, 12, 13 sts)

Cut yarn, leaving a 6-inch tail.

Thread tail through rem sts, pull tight and secure.

Thumb

Sl sts from holder back to needle.

Continuing Stripe Pattern, rejoin yarn and work even in St st for 8 (10, 12, 14) rows, ending with a WS row.

Next row (RS): K2tog across. (6, 7, 8, 8 sts)

Cut yarn leaving a 6-inch tail.

Thread tail through rem sts, pull tight and secure.

Sew side and thumb seams, being careful to line up stripes.

Weave in all ends.

Felting

Follow basic felting instructions on page 168 until finished measurements are obtained or mittens are desired size. ✱

Two-Tone Cuff Mittens

VERTICAL STRIPES ON THE CUFF AND A FUN CROCHETED FLOWER WILL MAKE THESE MITTENS STAND OUT IN ANY CROWD.

DESIGN BY SARA LOUISE HARPER

EASY

Sizes

Child's small (child's large, adult's small, adult's large) Instructions are given for smallest size, with larger sizes in parentheses. When only 1 number is given, it applies to all sizes.

Finished Felted Measurements

Wrist circumference: Approx 6¾ (7½, 8, 8¾) inches
Measurement achieved using yarn and colors specified; results may vary depending on yarn, yarn color and felting time.

Materials

- Plymouth Galway Worsted and Galway Worsted Highland Heather 100 percent wool medium weight yarn (210 yds/100g per ball):
    Child's: 1 ball each purple heather #743 (MC) and pink #135 (CC)
    Adult's: 2 balls each blue #15 (MC) and mint #111 (CC)
- Size 11 (8mm) straight needles or size needed to obtain gauge
- Stitch holder
- Stitch markers
- Size H/8 (5mm) crochet hook (optional)
- Tapestry needle

Pre-Felted Gauge

15 sts and 16 rows = 4 inches/10cm in St st

Exact gauge is not critical; make sure your sts are loose and airy.

Special Abbreviations

M1 (Make 1): Insert tip of LH needle under horizontal strand between st just worked and next st and k1-tbl.

Pm (place marker): Place marker on needle.

Sm (slip marker): Slip marker to other needle

Pattern Notes

Left and right mittens are worked the same.

For a smoother seam, sl first st of every row wyif. (This will not be repeated on every row.)

Mitten

Cuff

With MC, cast on 30 (34, 36, 40) sts.

Row 1: *K2 MC, k2 CC; rep from *, ending either k2 MC or k2 CC.

Row 2 and all WS rows: Purl colors in order established.

Rep [Rows 1 and 2] 11 (12, 12, 13) times, and *at the same time*, inc 1 st on each edge on 3rd row; [inc 1 st every 4th row] 5 times. (40, 44, 46, 50 sts)

Cut CC.

Using MC only, work 2 rows St st.

Thumb Gusset

Row 1 (RS): K19 (21, 22, 24), pm, M1, k2, M1, pm, k19 (21, 22, 24). (42, 46, 48, 52 sts)

Row 2 and all WS rows: Purl.

Row 3: Knit to marker, sm, M1, knit to next marker, M1, sm, knit to end.

Rep Rows 2 and 3 until there are 12 (14, 16, 16) sts between markers, ending with Row 2. (50, 56, 60, 64 sts)

Next row (RS): Knit to marker, place thumb sts on holder, knit to end. (40, 44, 46, 50 sts)

Hand

Work even for 21 (25, 27 33) rows, ending with a WS row.

Shape Top

Row 1 (RS): K0 (0, 2, 2), *k2tog, k2; rep from * to end of row. (30, 33, 35, 38 sts)

Row 2 and WS rows: Purl.

Row 3: K2tog 0 (0, 1, 1) time(s); *k1, k2tog; rep from * to end of row. (20, 22, 23, 25 sts)

Row 5: *K2tog across row, end k0 (0, 1, 1). (10, 11, 12, 13 sts)

Cut yarn, leaving a 6-inch tail.

Thread tail through rem sts; pull tight and secure.

Thumb

Sl sts from holder back to needle.

Rejoin yarn, and work even in St st for 8 (10, 12, 14) rows, ending with a WS row.

Next row (RS): K2tog across. (6, 7, 8, 8 sts)

Cut yarn, leaving a 6-inch tail.

Thread tail through rem sts and pull tight; secure on WS.

Sew side and thumb seams.

Weave in all ends.

Felting

Follow basic felting instructions on page 168 until finished measurements are obtained or mittens are desired size.

Shape if necessary and allow to dry thoroughly.

Crocheted Flower (optional)

With crochet hook and CC, ch-6 and join in a ring.

Rnd 1: Work 14 sc in ring, sl st to first sc at beg of rnd to close.

Rnd 2: [Work sc, ch 6, sc into back lp] in each of the 14 sc.

Rnd 3: [Work sc, ch 4, sc into front lp] in each of the 14 sc; sl st to first sc, then fasten off, leaving a long tail to sew flower to mitten.

Attach crocheted flower by tacking down in several spots—do not allow flower to lose its dimension. ✳

Winter Fun Mittens

BASIC MITTENS FOR THE WHOLE FAMILY— EASY TO KNIT, FELTED FOR WARMTH.

DESIGN BY SARA LOUISE HARPER

EASY

Sizes
Child's small (child's large, adult's small, adult's large) Instructions are given for smallest size, with larger sizes in parentheses. When only 1 number is given, it applies to all sizes.

Finished Felted Measurement
Wrist circumference: Approx 6¾ (7½, 8, 8¾) inches
Measurement achieved using yarn and color specified; results may vary depending on yarn, yarn color and felting time.

Materials
- Plymouth Outback Wool 100 percent wool medium weight yarn (370 yds/200g per skein):
  Child's: 1 skein orange variegated #913
  Adult's: 1 skein purple variegated #959
- Size 9 (5.5mm) straight needles or size needed to obtain gauge
- Stitch holder
- Stitch markers
- Tapestry needle

Pre-Felted Gauge
15 sts and 16 rows = 4 inches/10cm in St st
Exact gauge is not critical; make sure your sts are loose and airy.

Special Abbreviation
M1 (Make 1): Insert tip of LH needle under horizontal strand between st just worked and next st and k1-tbl.
Pm (place marker): Place marker on needle.

Sm (slip marker): Slip marker to other needle.

Pattern Notes
Left and right mittens are worked the same.

For a smoother seam, sl first st of every row wyif. (This will not be repeated on every row.)

Mitten

Cuff

Cast on 30 (34, 36, 40) sts.

Working in St st throughout mitten, inc 2 sts evenly [every 4th row] 5 times (40, 44, 46, 50 sts total). Work 5 rows even.

Thumb Gusset

Row 1 (RS): K19 (21, 22, 24), pm, M1, k2, M1, pm, k19 (21, 22, 24). (42, 46, 48, 52 sts)

Row 2 and all WS rows: Purl.

Row 3: Knit to marker, sm, M1, knit to next marker, M1, sm, knit to end.

Rep Rows 2 and 3 until there are 12 (14, 16, 16) sts between markers, ending with Row 2. (50, 56, 60, 64 sts)

Next row (RS): Knit to marker, place thumb sts on holder, knit to end. (40, 44, 46, 50 sts)

Hand

Work even for 21 (25, 27 33) rows, ending with a WS row.

Shape Top

Row 1 (RS): K0 (0, 2, 2), *k2tog, k2; rep from * to end of row. (30, 33, 35, 38 sts)

Row 2 and WS rows: Purl.

Row 3: K2tog 0 (0, 1, 1) time(s); *k1, k2tog; rep from * to end of row. (20, 22, 23, 25 sts)

Row 5: *K2tog across row, end k0 (0, 1, 1). (10, 11, 12, 13 sts)

Cut yarn, leaving a 6-inch tail.

Thread tail through rem sts; pull tight and secure.

Thumb

Sl sts from holder back to needle.

Rejoin yarn and work even in St st for 8 (10, 12, 14) rows, ending with a WS row.

Next row (RS): K2tog across. (6, 7, 8, 8 sts)

Cut yarn leaving a 6-inch tail.

Thread tail through rem sts and pull tight; secure on WS.

Sew side and thumb seams.

Weave in all ends.

Felting

Follow basic felting instructions on page 168 until finished measurements are obtained or mittens are desired size.

Shape if necessary, and allow to dry thoroughly. ✻

Shades of Blue Wristers

THESE WRISTERS ARE DESIGNED TO KEEP YOUR FINGERS FREE WHILE KEEPING YOUR PULSE-POINTS WARM.

DESIGN BY LAURA ANDERSSON

EASY

Size

Woman's average

Finished Felted Measurement

Wrist circumference: Approx 6½ inches

Measurement achieved using yarns and colors specified; results may vary depending on yarn, yarn color and felting time.

Materials

- Plymouth Eros 100 percent nylon medium weight yarn (165 yds/50g per ball): 1 ball purple #3267 (A) **4 MEDIUM**
- Plymouth Alpaca Bouclé 90 percent alpaca/10 percent nylon super bulky weight yarn (70 yds/50g per ball): 1 ball blue #20 (B) **6 SUPER BULKY**
- Plymouth Galway Worsted 100 percent wool medium weight yarn (210 yds/100g per ball): 1 ball each light teal #139 (C) and dark teal #116 (D)
- Size 9 double-pointed needles or size needed to obtain gauge
- Stitch marker
- Crochet hook or tapestry needle

Pre-Felted Gauge

14 sts and 18 rows = 4 inches/10cm in St st with 2 strands held tog

Exact gauge is not critical; make sure your sts are loose and airy.

Pattern Note

This wrister is worked in bands of different st patterns and yarn combinations (A and B, A and D, or single strand of C) which felt at different rates. This helps create the shaping of the finished wrister.

Wrister

Ruffle Band

With 1 strand each of A and B held tog, cast on 90 sts.

Knit 1 row, then join without twisting; place marker between first and last sts.

Rnds 1, 3 and 5: Knit.

Rnds 2 and 4: *K2tog, k1; rep from * around. (40 sts)

Rnd 6: *K2tog, k2; rep from * around. (30 sts)

Work even until ruffle measures 3 inches from beg. Cut A and B.

Main Wrister Band

Join C.

Rnd 1: *K1, knit 1 in front and back, rep from * to last 2 sts, k2. (44 sts)

Work in k2, p2 rib for 5 inches. Cut C.

Bracelet Band

Join 1 strand each A and D.

Work in garter st for 8 rows.

Final Rib Band

With A and D, work in k2, p2 rib for 1½ inches.

Bind off purlwise.

Weave in ends, working each color into same-colored band.

Felting

Follow basic felting instructions on page 168 until finished measurements are obtained or wristers are desired size, or slightly larger. Retain the ribbing in the long middle section, but there should be some hazy softening of the st definition. ✳

{ Cozy Feet: Slippers }

WHEN TEMPERATURES DROP, SLIP YOUR FEET
INTO A PAIR OF KNIT AND FELTED SLIPPERS.

Fair Isle Slipper Socks

GIVE YOUR TOES THE ROYAL TREATMENT WITH THESE WONDERFULLY PATTERNED SOCKS.

DESIGN BY GAYLE BUNN

INTERMEDIATE

Size
Woman's average

Finished Felted Measurement
Leg circumference: 10 inches
Measurement achieved using yarn and colors specified; results may vary depending on yarn, yarn color and felting time.

Materials
- Plymouth Galway Worsted 100 percent wool medium weight yarn (210 yds/100g per ball): 2 balls black #9 (MC) and 1 ball each of ivory #1 (A), green #130 (B) and fuchsia #117 (C)
- Size 8 (5mm) double-pointed needles (5) or size to obtain gauge
- Stitch marker
- Tapestry needle

Gauge
19 sts and 25 rows = 4 inches/10cm in St st
Exact gauge is not critical; make sure your sts are loose and airy.

Special Abbreviations
N1 (Needle 1)
N2 (Needle 2)
N3 (Needle 3)
N4 (Needle 4)

Slipper Socks
Leg
Using cable cast-on method, *cast on 1 MC, cast on 1 A; rep from * 27 times. (56 sts)
Cut A.
Distribute sts evenly on 4 dpns (14 sts on each needle). Join without twisting, place marker between first and last sts.
With MC, knit 8 rnds.
Next 8 rnds: Work Chart A around.
With B, knit 3 rnds.
Next 6 rnds: Work Chart B around.
With B, knit 3 rnds.
Next 8 rnds: Work Chart A around.
With MC, knit 3 rnds.
Next 15 rnds: Work Chart C around.
With MC, knit 1 rnd dec 4 sts evenly around. (52 sts, 13 sts on each needle)

Heel Flap
Sl sts from N4 to N1 for heel. (26 sts)
With WS facing, join MC to 26 heel sts and beg with a purl row, work back and forth in St st until heel measures 2½ inches, ending with a RS row.

Turn Heel
Row 1 (WS): Sl 1, p14, p2tog, p1, turn.
Row 2: Sl 1, k4, ssk, k1, turn.
Row 3: Sl 1, p5, p2tog, p1, turn.
Row 4: Sl 1, k6, ssk, k1, turn.
Row 5: Sl 1, p7, p2tog, p1, turn.
Row 6: Sl 1, k8, ssk, k1, turn.
Row 7: Sl 1, p9, p2tog, p1, turn.
Row 8: Sl 1, k10, ssk, k1, turn.
Row 9: Sl 1, p11, p2tog, turn.
Row 10: Sl 1, k12, ssk, k1, turn. (14 sts)

Gusset & Foot
Pick-up rnd (RS): N1 (needle holding heel sts): pick up and knit 14 sts along left side of heel; N2 and N3: knit; N4: pick up and knit 14 sts along right side of heel, then knit the first 7 sts on N1; place marker for beg of rnd. (68 sts arranged 21-13-13-21)
Rnd 1: N1: knit to last 2 sts, k2tog; N2 and N3: knit; N4: ssk, knit to end. (66 sts)
Rnd 2: Knit around.
[Rep Rnds 1 and 2] 7 times. (52 sts, 13 on each needle)
Work even until foot measures 6½ inches from pick-up rnd.

Toe
Rnd 1: *N1: knit to last 3 sts, k2tog, k1; N2: k1, ssk, knit to end; N3 and N4: rep from *. (48 sts)
Rnd 2: Knit around.
[Rep Rnds 1 and 2] 6 times. (24 sts)
Sl sts from N4 to N1 and from N2 to N3. Holding N1 and N3 parallel, graft sts using Kitchener st (see page 173).

Felting
Follow basic felting instructions on page 168 until finished measurements are obtained or slippers are desired size. Shape, then stuff with hand towel to dry. ✽

COLOR KEY
- ◼ Black (MC)
- ☐ Ivory (A)
- ◼ Green (B)
- ◼ Fuchsia

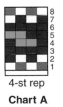

8
7
6
5
4
3
2
1

4-st rep

Chart A

6
5
4
3
2
1

4-st rep

Chart B

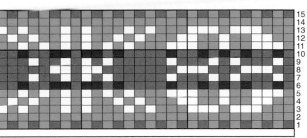

15
14
13
12
11
10
9
8
7
6
5
4
3
2
1

28-st rep

Chart C

Elves in Many Sizes

THESE WONDERFUL ELF SLIPPERS USE A COMBINATION OF WOOL, NOVELTY YARN AND GARTER STITCH TO CREATE A THICK, TEXTURED FABRIC WHICH CAN BE SHAPED AFTER FELTING.

DESIGN BY CHRISTINE WALTER

EASY

Sizes
Approx shoe size: infant's 5–6 (child's 10, child's 1–2, woman's 5–6, woman's 8–9) Instructions are given for smallest size, with larger sizes in parentheses. When only 1 number is given, it applies to all sizes.

Finished Felted Measurements
Foot length: Approx 5 (6½, 8, 9, 10) inches

Measurements achieved using yarns and colors specified; results may vary depending on yarn, yarn color and felting time.

Materials
- Plymouth Combolo 66 percent nylon/30 percent tactel/4 percent polyester bulky weight yarn (47 yds/50g per ball): 2 (3, 3, 4, 4) balls lilac #1055 *or* green #1031 (A)
- Plymouth Galway Worsted 100 percent wool medium weight yarn (210 yds/100g per ball): 1 (1, 1, 1, 2) balls lavender #89 *or* olive green #106 (B)
- Size 11 (8mm) straight needles or size needed to obtain gauge
- Tapestry needle

Pre-Felted Gauge
11 sts and 22 rows = 4 inches/10cm in garter st with A and B held tog
Exact gauge is not critical; make sure your sts are loose and airy.

Special Abbreviation
K1f&b (knit 1 forward and back): Inc 1 st by knitting in front and back of st.

Pattern Notes
One strand each of A and B are held tog throughout.

There is little difference between unfelted and felted gauge.

These slippers will be custom-fit by blocking the felted item on the actual foot. In this way, each size can be adjusted to fit a range of feet.

Slippers
With 1 strand each of A and B held tog, cast on 31 (39, 49, 53, 61) sts.
Row 1 (WS): Knit.
Row 2: K1f&b, k13 (17, 22, 24, 28), k3tog, k12 (16, 21, 23, 27), k1f&b, k1.
Rep [Rows 1 and 2] 2 (2, 3, 3, 4) times.

Shape Foot
Row 1 and every WS row: Knit.
Row 2: K14 (18, 23, 25, 29), k3tog, k14 (18, 23, 25, 29).
Row 4: K13 (17, 22, 24, 28), k3tog, k13 (17, 22, 24, 28).
Continue dec in this manner every other row until 7 sts rem (slipper toe).
Knit 1 row.
Cut yarn, leaving a 6-inch tail.
Thread tail through the rem sts, pull tight and secure.

Finishing
Sew seam from toe to back of heel. Weave in ends.

Felting
Felt either by hand or machine, following basic felting instructions on page 168 until finished measurements are obtained or slippers are desired size.

Shape and block slippers by putting them on the intended wearer's feet and shaping to desired size. You can also make the toe more or less pointy while the fabric is wet. Remove carefully; stuff and allow to dry. ✳

Child's Footies

THESE FOOTIES, WHICH ARE SO EASY TO KNIT, WILL KEEP LITTLE TOES WARM AND COZY ON THE COLDEST WINTER DAY!

DESIGN BY SARA LOUISE HARPER

EASY

Sizes

Approx shoe size: child's 5–7 (8–10, 11–13, 1–3) Instructions are given for smallest size, with larger sizes in parentheses. When only 1 number is given, it applies to all sizes.

Finished Felted Measurement

Heel-to-toe: Approx 6 (7, 8, 9) inches
Measurement achieved using yarn and color specified; results may vary depending on yarn, yarn color and felting time.

Materials

- Plymouth Hand Paint Wool 100 percent wool bulky weight yarn (66 yds/100g per skein): 2 (2, 3, 3) skeins blue/purple variegated #150
- Size 17 (12mm) straight needles or size needed to obtain gauge
- Tapestry needle
- Size K/10.5 (6.5mm) crochet hook
- 2 (20-inch) lengths lavender ribbon
- Puff paint (optional)

Pre-Felted Gauge

10 sts and 9 rows = 4 inches/10cm in St st
Exact gauge is not critical; make sure your sts are loose and airy.

Footies

Cast on 27 (30, 32, 35) sts, leaving a long tail for seaming.

Row 1 (RS): K8 (9, 10, 11), p1, k9 (10, 10, 11), p1, k8 (9, 10, 11).
Row 2: P8 (9, 10, 11), k1, p9 (10, 10, 11), k1, p8 (9, 10, 11).
Rep Rows 1 and 2 until piece measures approx 6 (6¾, 7¾, 8¾) inches, ending with a RS row. Knit 3 rows.
Next row (RS): *K1, ssk, knit to last 3 sts, k2tog, k1. (25, 28, 30, 33 sts)
Next row: Purl across.*
Rep from * to * 4 times. (17, 20, 22, 25 sts)
Next row: K1 (0, 0, 1), *k2tog; rep from * across. (9, 10, 11, 13 sts)
Cut yarn, leaving a 15-inch tail. Thread tail through the rem sts, pull tight and secure.

Assembly

Use ending tail to seam top foot up to and including the garter rows.
Use cast-on tail to seam back of footie. Starting at top, sew down to rev St sts, then fold bottom of footie up to form an upside down "T."
Weave in all ends.

Felting

Felt either by hand or machine, following basic felting instructions on page 168 until finished measurements are obtained or footies are desired size.
Shape, then allow to dry thoroughly.

Finishing

Add ribbon embellishment by pulling ribbon through to front with a crochet hook. Tie in bow.
Dot or stripe the bottom with puff paint to make them nonskid, especially for small children. ❋

Mary Jane Slippers

YOUR LITTLE GIRL WILL FEEL OH-SO-SPECIAL WEARING HER PRETTY, LITTLE FELTED MARY JANES.

DESIGN BY SCARLET TAYLOR

BEGINNER

Size
Child's shoe size 8½–9½

Finished Felted Measurements
4 inches x 9½ inches
Measurements achieved using yarn and colors specified; results may vary depending on yarn, yarn color and felting time.

Materials
- Plymouth Baby Alpaca DK 100 percent baby alpaca lightweight yarn (125 yds/50g per ball): 1 ball each light tan #207 (A), dark tan #208 (B), blue #4148 (C), lavender #1830 (D) and dark purple #1810 (E)
- Size 8 (5mm) knitting needles
- Size 10 (6mm) straight needles or size needed to obtain gauge.
- Tapestry needle
- 2 (5/8-inch) shank buttons
- Nonskid stickers to apply to bottom of slippers (optional)

Pre-Felted Gauge
18 sts and 24 rows = 4 inches/10cm in St st with larger needles
Exact gauge is not critical; make sure your sts are loose and airy.

Special Abbreviation
M1 (Make 1): Insert LH needle front to back under the strand between the 2 needles; knit the strand tbl to inc 1 st.

Pattern Notes
Slippers are made in 1 piece, then joined with side seams.
Knit your gauge swatch in the same color you would like your buttons. Felt, then set aside to use later for covering buttons.

Slipper
Upper Instep
With larger needles and B, cast on 36 sts.
Work in St st for 3 inches, ending with a WS row.
Cut B.

Shape Upper Toe
Join A and work 4 rows even in St st.
Dec row (RS): Ssk, knit to last 2 sts, k2tog. (34 sts)
[Rep dec row every other row] 10 times. (14 sts)
Purl 1 row.

Shape Lower Toe
Inc row (RS): K1, M1, knit to last st, M1, k1. (16 sts)
[Rep inc row every other row] 9 times, then [every 4th row] once, ending with a WS row. (36 sts)
Cut A.

Striped Sole
Continue working in St st, work 18 rows B, 18 rows C, then 18 rows D, cutting each yarn when done with stripe.

Shape Heel
Join E.
Work Dec row on next, then [every 4th row] twice, then [every other row] 6 times, ending with a WS row. (18 sts)

Upper Heel
Work Inc row [every other row] 6 times, then [every 4th row] 3 times, ending with a WS row. (36 sts) Cut E.

Shape Foot Opening
Join D.
Next row (RS): K5, join a 2nd ball of D and bind off center 26 sts, k5. (5 sts each side)
Working both sides at once with separate balls of yarn, work even for 17 more rows. Cut D.
Join C and work 12 rows even.
Work Inc row [every other row] twice, then [every row] twice. (9 sts each side)
Bind off.
Fold upper slipper at toe and heel, and sew side seams.
With RS facing, smaller needles and A, pick up and knit 90 sts around foot opening. Bind off knitwise.

Strap
Right Slipper Strap
With RS facing and smaller needles, pick up and knit 7 sts on left side of slipper.

Work in garter st until strap measures
 6¼ inches.
Bind off.

Left Slipper Strap
Work as for right slipper strap, but
 pick up strap sts on RS of slipper.
Weave in all ends.

Felting
Follow basic felting instructions
 on page 168 until finished
 measurements are obtained or
 slippers are desired size.

Finishing
With A, make a button loop on end
 of each strap.
Cut a small circle of felted fabric from
 swatch to fit around button and
 sew edges tog to secure.
Sew button on slipper opposite loop.
Apply nonskid stickers to bottom of
 each slipper, if desired. ✳

Great Carriers: Purses & Totes

WE HAVE CLASSY AND SASSY STYLES, BOTH LARGE AND SMALL, TO CARRY EVERY DAY OR TO TAKE FOR A NIGHT ON THE TOWN.

Thinking on the Bright Side

KNIT AND CROCHET COMBINE TO MAKE A FAVORITE BEACH BAG. STUFF YOUR SHELLS IN THE SHELL-SHAPED POCKET AS YOU WALK ALONG THE BEACH.

DESIGN BY ANITA CLOSIC

INTERMEDIATE

Finished Felted Measurements

16 inches wide x 11 inches deep
Measurements achieved using yarns
and colors specified; results may
vary depending on yarn, yarn color
and felting time.

Materials

- Plymouth Galway Worsted
  100 percent wool medium
  weight yarn (210 yds/100g
  per ball): 4 balls gold #60 (A)
- Plymouth Eros 100 percent nylon
  medium weight yarn (165 yds/50g
  per ball): 1 ball brown #4132 (B)
- Plymouth Margarita 78 percent
  nylon/22 percent micro tactel
  medium weight yarn (88 yds/50g
  per ball): 1 ball red #3535 (C)
- Plymouth Daiquiri 70 percent
  nylon/30 percent cotton medium
  weight yarn (93 yds/50g per ball): 1
  ball red #3535 (D)
- Plymouth Baby Alpaca Grande 100
  percent baby alpaca bulky weight
  yarn (110 yds/100g per skein): 1
  skein pale green #1310 (E)
- Size 13 (9mm) double-pointed
  needles and 24-inch circular needle
  or size needed to obtain gauge
- Size I/9 (5.5mm) crochet hook
- Size K/10½ (6.5mm) crochet hook
- Tapestry needle
- Stitch markers (1 in contrasting
  color for beg of rnd)
- 6¾-inch-diameter bamboo-type
  purse handles #SFPH-B01 from

Sunbelt Fastener
- Small piece driftwood for
  embellishment (optional)

Gauge

12 sts and 16 rnds = 4 inches in St st
  with 2 strands A held tog
Exact gauge is not critical; make sure
  your sts are loose and airy.

Special Abbreviations

K1f&b (knit 1 front and back): Inc 1
  by knitting in front and back of st.

Pattern Notes

Bag is worked holding 2 strands A
  tog throughout.

Bag
Base

With dpns and 2 strands A held tog,
  cast on 6 sts.
Distribute evenly on 3 needles.
Join without twisting; place marker
  between first and last sts.
Rnd 1: K1f&b in every st around.
  (12 sts)

Rnd 2 and all even numbered rnds: Purl.

Rnd 3: *K1, k1f&b, place marker; rep from * around. (18 sts)

Inc rnd: *Knit to 1 st before marker, k1f&b; rep from * around. (24 sts)

Rep Inc rnd [every other rnd] 9 times, changing to circular needle when necessary. (78 sts)

Purl 1 rnd, knit 1 rnd, purl 1 rnd.

Sides

*Beg St st (knit all rnds) and work even for 3 inches.

Next rnd: Work Inc rnd. (84 sts)*

Rep from * to * 4 times. (108 sts)

[Purl 1 rnd, knit 1 rnd] twice, purl 1 rnd.

Bind off purlwise.

Weave in ends.

Shell Pocket

With larger crochet hook and 2 strands A held tog, ch 4, join with sl st in first ch. Mark beg of rnd.

Note: *Following rnds are worked in back lps only. Do not join. Spiral forms as rnds are worked.*

Rnd 1: Work 8 sc in ring.

Rnd 2: [2 hdc in next sc] 5 times, [2 dc in next sc] 3 times. (16 sts)

Rnd 3: [2 dc in next hdc] 6 times, [2 tr in next hdc] 4 times, [2 tr in next dc] 3 times, tr in next dc, 2 tr in next dc, tr in next dc.

Rnd 4: 2 tr in next dc, [tr in next dc, 2 tr in next dc] 5 times, tr in next dc, [2 tr in next tr, tr in next tr] 8 times.

Continuing in spiral, *tr in next st, 2 tr in next st; rep from * until shell measures 6 inches in diameter. Fasten off.

With 2 strands B held tog and beg at the center of the spiral, sc into the front lp of each st around the spiral. Fasten off.

Sew onto front of bag, leaving top half open for pocket.

Leaf

Make 2

With smaller crochet hook and E, ch 16. Turn.

Rnd 1: Working in back lp only, sl st in each ch.

Rnd 2: Ch 4, working in unused lps of beg ch, dc in 2nd unused lp, ch 1, sk next lp, dc in next lp, [ch 2, sk next lp, tr in next lp] twice, [ch 2, sk next lp, dtr in next lp] twice, ch 2, sk next lp, ttr in next lp ch 7, sk next lp, sc in next, working along opposite side in sl sts, sc in first sl st, ch 7, sk 1 sl st, ttr in next sl st, [ch 2, sk next sl st, dtr in next sl st] twice, [ch 2, sk next sl st, tr in next sl st] twice, ch 2, sl next sl st, dc in next sl st, ch 1, sk next sl st, dc in next sl st, ch 3, sl st in first ch of beg ch-4.

Rnd 3: Ch 1, *dc over next ch, sc in next st; rep from * around, sl st in beg ch.

Weave in ends.

Flower

With smaller crochet hook and 1 strand each of C and D held tog, ch 8, join with sl st to form ring.

Rnd 1: Work 8 sc in center of ring, join with sl st to first sc.

Rnd 2 (form petal): *Ch 8, sc into next sc, rep from * around, join to first ch 8 with sl st.

Rnd 3: *Sl st 4 to center of first petal, ch 4 and sc in back lp of sc between the petals, ch 4 and sc in back lp of the center of the petal; rep from * around all petals, join with sl st to sc. Fasten off.

Weave in ends.

Do not felt.

Felting

Turn bag inside out.

With leaves and bag in separate bags, follow basic felting instructions on page 168 until finished measurements are obtained or bag is desired size.

Shape and stuff to dry.

After completely dry, carefully trim excess fuzziness with scissors to smooth surface appearance.

Finishing

Sew flower and felted leaves to front of bag (see photo).

Attach driftwood (optional).

Attach handles. ✳

Plaid for Your Possessions

YOU'LL FEEL JUST A LITTLE BIT SCOTTISH TOTING THIS LOVELY TARTAN BAG. IT EVEN HAS A MATCHING CHANGE PURSE.

DESIGNS BY GAYLE BUNN

EXPERIENCED

Finished Felted Measurements

Bag: 17 inches wide x 13½ inches deep

Change purse: 6½ x 4 inches
Measurements achieved using yarn and colors specified; results may vary depending on yarn, yarn color and felting time.

Materials
For both projects
- Plymouth Galway Worsted  100 percent wool medium weight yarn (210 yds/100g per ball): 1 ball each red #44 (MC), ivory #1 (A), black #9 (B), green #130 (C) and gold #60 (D)
- Size 7 (4.5mm) straight and double-pointed needles (4) or size needed to obtain gauge
- 6-inch zipper for change purse
- ¾ yard of lining fabric
- Sewing machine

Pre-Felted Gauge
20 sts and 26 rows = 4 inches/10cm in St st
Exact gauge is not critical; make sure your sts are loose and airy.

Pattern Notes
This bag is worked combining intarsia and Fair Isle methods. Use separate lengths of yarn for each horizontal stripe, working Fair Isle method on the black (B) and gold (D) rows.
The vertical dots in green (C) and gold (D) are worked in duplicate st (see photo) after the bag is knit.

Duplicate Stitch
Pull yarn through to front. Place needle from right to left behind both sides of the stitch above the one being duplicated. Complete the stitch by returning needle to where you began.

Bag
Front & Back
Make 2
With straight needles and MC, cast on 101 sts.
Work Rows 1–28 of Chart 4 times; work Rows 1–10.
Bind off with MC.
With C and D, work vertical stripes in duplicate st following Chart.

Handles
Make 2
With dpns and B, cast on 12 sts.

Distribute sts evenly on 3 dpns. Join without twisting; place marker between first and last sts.
Knit in rnds until piece measures 23 inches.
Bind off loosely.

Change Purse
Front & Back
Make 2
With MC, cast on 37 sts.
Work Rows 7–28 of Chart; work Rows 1–6.
Bind off with MC.

Work vertical stripes with C and D in duplicate st.

Felting

Using tapestry needle, weave a length of MC through bind-off edge of front and back pieces of bag so edge measures approx 18 inches (this will keep top edge of bag secure during felting process). Follow basic felting instructions on page 168 until finished measurements are obtained or bag is desired size. Dry flat.

Bag Assembly
Lining

Using front or back of bag as a guide, trace shape onto lining fabric, leaving a ½-inch border along top

edge for fold back. Cut out 2 lining pieces. With sewing machine, sew outer seam of lining pieces tog using a ½-inch seam allowance. Press remaining top edge of lining to WS along seam allowance.

With sewing machine, sew sides and lower edge of tote bag front and back using a ½-inch seam allowance. St each corner diagonally to form base of bag. Trim corners. Sew folded edge of lining to top inner edge of bag.

Sew open ends of handles closed and sew each end to back and front as shown in photo.

Change-Purse Assembly
Lining

Using front or back of change purse

as a guide, trace shape onto lining fabric, leaving a ½-inch border along top edge for fold back. Cut out 2 lining pieces. With sewing machine, sew outer seam of lining pieces tog using a ½-inch seam allowance. Press rem top edge of lining to WS along seam allowance.

Pin zipper in position under bind-off edges of front and back. With sewing machine, sew zipper in position, then sides and lower edge of change-purse front and back using a ½-inch seam allowance. Sew folded edge of lining to top inner edge of change purse (this is easiest to do when the change purse is turned inside out). ✳

COLOR KEY
- ■ Red (MC)
- □ Ivory (A)
- ■ Black (B)
- ■ Green (C)
- ■ Gold (D)
- ■ When knitting, work in adjacent color; duplicate st in C
- ■ When knitting, work in adjacent color; duplicate st in D

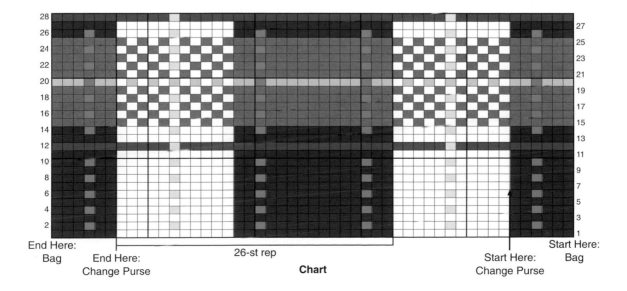

End Here: Bag

End Here: Change Purse

26-st rep

Chart

Start Here: Change Purse

Start Here: Bag

Flirtatious Bag

THIS BAG IS JUST WHAT YOU NEED FOR A NIGHT ON THE TOWN. WE SHOW A SHORT WRIST STRAP, BUT BY MAKING A LONGER I-CORD YOU COULD MAKE A SHOULDER STRAP.

DESIGN BY ELLEN EDWARDS DRECHSLER

EASY

Finished Felted Measurements

10 inches wide x 8½ inches deep
Measurements achieved using yarns and colors specified; results may vary depending on yarn, yarn color and felting time.

Materials

- Plymouth Galway Worsted 100 percent wool medium weight yarn (210 yds/100g per ball): 4 balls beige #138 (A)

  4 MEDIUM

- Plymouth Hot! Hot! Hot! 65 percent nylon/30 percent polyester/5 percent acrylic super bulky weight yarn (33 yds/50g per ball): 2 balls plum #681 (B)

  6 SUPER BULKY

- Size 13 (9mm) straight needles or size needed to obtain gauge
- Tapestry needle
- Size 4 metal snap
- Sharp sewing needle and thread to match yarn

Pre-Felted Gauge

7 sts and 9 rows = 4 inches/10cm in rev St st with 2 strands A and 1 strand B held tog
Exact gauge is not critical; make sure your sts are loose and airy.

Special Technique

I-cord: *K3, do not turn. Sl sts back to LH needle; rep from * until cord is desired length. Bind off.

Pattern Notes

The purl side is the RS of bag.
The bag is worked with multiple strands of yarn held tog; follow instructions accordingly.

Bag

With 2 strands A held tog, cast on 30 sts.
Knit 8 rows.
Add 1 strand B. Work in St st for 14 inches. Cut B.
Continue in St st with 2 strands A and knit 8 rows.

Bind off to last 3 sts.

Strap

Wrist strap

Work I-cord for 11 inches. Bind off.

Shoulder strap

Work I-cord until strap measures twice desired finished length. Bind off.

Assembly

Turn bag purl side out (this is RS). Sew side seams.

Wrist strap
Sew end of I-cord opposite side seam forming a small lp.

Shoulder strap
Sew end of I-cord to opposite corner of bag.
Use fingers or a crochet hook to gently pull strands of B to RS (purl side) of bag.

Felting
Place bag in pillowcase and follow basic felting instructions on page 168 until finished measurements are obtained or bag is desired size.

Shape to dry.

Finishing
Trim ribbon yarn as desired.
Sew a size 4 metal snap inside the bag for closure. ✳

Carry Your Laptop

YOUR LAPTOP CAN TRAVEL IN STYLE INSIDE THIS STURDY, STRIPED BAG. CHANGE COLORS TO MATCH YOUR PERSONALITY, WHETHER CONSERVATIVE OR A LITTLE FLAMBOYANT.

DESIGN BY DONNA DRUCHUNAS

INTERMEDIATE

Size
Small (medium, large) Instructions are given for smallest size, with larger sizes in parentheses. When only 1 number is given, it applies to all sizes.

Finished Felted Measurements
Approx 14 (17, 20) inches wide x 12 inches tall
Measurements achieved using yarn and color specified; results may vary depending on yarn, yarn color and felting time.

Materials

- Plymouth Galway Worsted 100 percent wool medium weight yarn (210 yds/100g per ball): 3 skeins purple #13 (A), 2 skeins mauve #19 (B), 1 skein persimmon #107 (C), 1 skein blue #15 (D)
- Size 15 (10mm) 24-inch circular needle or size needed to obtain gauge
- Size 15 (10mm) double-pointed needles (2)
- Tapestry needle

Pre-Felted Gauge
9 sts and 12 rows = 4 inches/10cm in St st holding 2 strands of yarn tog
Exact gauge is not critical; make sure your sts are loose and airy.

Special Techniques
A. I-cord: *K3, do not turn, sl sts back to LH needle; rep from *until cord is desired length. Bind off.
B. Attached I-cord: *Insert LH tip of dpn holding sts into the next edge st and slide sts to other end of dpn. K2, k2tog. Do not turn. Rep from * until all sts are worked.

Pattern Note
Hold 2 strands of yarn tog throughout.

Laptop Case
Sides
With 2 strands of A held tog, cast on 80 sts.
Work stripe pat in St st as follows: 6 rows A, 2 rows D, 4 rows B, 6 rows D, 2 rows C, 6 rows A, 4 rows B, 4 rows D, 2 rows C, 4 rows D, 8 rows B, 4 rows A, 4 rows C, 2 rows D, 2 rows C. Continue in stripes as indicated below.

Small
Continue with All Sizes.

Medium
Work 6 rows A, 4 rows B, 2 rows D.
Continue with All Sizes.

Large
Work 6 rows A, 4 rows B, 2 rows D, 8 rows B, 4 rows D.
Continue with All Sizes.

All Sizes
Work 6 rows A.

Bind off.
Fold piece in half with ends of stripes at top opening. Sew side seams.
Turn bag inside out. Sew a short seam across each bottom corner perpendicular to the side seam. Turn bag RS out.

Top Edge
With circular needle and A, pick up and knit 106 (126, 146) sts evenly around the top opening of the bag. Knit rnds until top edge measures 4 inches.

Straps
With dpns and 2 strands A held tog, cast on 3 sts.
Beg at side seam, work attached I-cord around entire top edge of bag.
Mark center 8 inches of front and back with pins.
With dpns and 2 strands B held tog, cast on 3 sts.
*Beg at side seam, work attached I-cord to the first pin, work 8 inches of unattached I-cord, beg at 2nd pin, work attached I-cord to side seam; rep from * once. Bind off.
With dpns and 2 strands of B held tog, cast on 3 sts. Beg at side seam, work attached I-cord around entire top edge of bag.
With dpns and 3 strands A held tog, cast on 3 sts. Beg at side seam, work attached I-cord around entire top edge of bag.

Sew ends of I-cord pieces tog at
side seam.
Weave in ends.

Felting
Follow basic felting instructions
on page 168 until finished

measurements are obtained or case
is desired size. Shape to dry. ✱

Rainbow Project Bag

NO ONE SHOULD EVER BE ON THE ROAD WITHOUT
KNITTING SUPPLIES. TAKE YOUR PROJECTS WITH
YOU IN THIS OPTIMISTIC TOTE BAG.

DESIGN BY CINDY ADAMS

EASY

Finished Felted Measurements

24 inches across top (opened wide) x
12 inches deep

Measurements achieved using yarn
and colors specified; results may
vary depending on yarn, yarn color
and felting time.

Materials

- Plymouth Galway Worsted
100 percent wool medium
weight yarn (210 yds/100g
per ball): 2 balls each red #16 (A),
orange #91 (B), gold #60 (C), green
#130 (D), aqua #116 (E), navy #10
(F) and purple #30 (G)
- Size 11 (8mm) 36-inch circular
needle or size needed to obtain
gauge
- Stitch markers, 1 in contrasting
color for beg of rnd
- Cotton waste yarn
- Sewing thread to match G
- Sharp sewing needle

Pre-Felted Gauge

10 sts and 12 rnds = 4 inches/10cm in
St st holding 2 strands tog

Exact gauge is not critical; make sure
your sts are loose and airy.

Special Abbreviation

Pm (place marker): Place marker
on needle.

Special Technique

I-cord: *K5, do not turn, sl sts back to
LH needle; rep from * until cord is
desired length. Bind off.

Pattern Notes

Bag is worked with 2 strands of yarn
held tog throughout.

To prevent a jog at the side, change
colors in different places on each
color-change rnd, alternating
between a few sts before and a few
sts after beg-of-rnd marker.

Bag

Base

With 2 strands A held tog, cast on
48 sts.

Knit 38 rows.

Sides

Pick-up rnd: K48, pm, pick up and
knit 19 sts along side, pm, 48 sts
along cast-on edge, pm, and 19 sts
along rem side, pm for beg of rnd.
(134 sts)

Working St st in the rnd (knit every
rnd), and working with 2 strands of
yarn held tog, work stripes as follows:

4 rnds with 2 A.
3 rnds with A and B.
5 rnds with 2 B.
2 rnds with B and C.
3 rnds with 2 C.
3 rnds with C and D.
4 rnds with 2 D.

3 rnds with D and E.
5 rnds with 2 E.
4 rnds with E and F.
7 rnds with 2 F.
7 rnds with F and G.
6 rnds with 2 G.

K48, bind off rem sts. As you bind off,
tie a short length of cotton yarn or
thread at the marked positions.

Flap

Working back and forth in St st on
rem 48 sts, work the stripe pat in
reverse, beg with 6 rows with 2 G
and ending with 2 A. Bind off.

Weave in all ends.

Handle

With G, cast on 5 sts and work 80
inches of I-cord.

Felting

Putting pieces in separate bags, felt
bag and handle following basic
felting instructions on page 168
until finished measurements are
obtained or bag is desired size.

Finishing

Cut the handle in half, making sure
that the pieces are the same
length. Position the ends of handles
on RS of bag at cotton markers
with approx 1 inch overlapping.

Sew the handles on the bag, removing
markers before sewing. ✱

My Blue Checkerboard

A TOP EDGING OF SPARKLY YARN ADDS A FESTIVE TOUCH TO THIS CHECKERBOARD-VARIATION PURSE.

DESIGN BY ELLEN EDWARDS DRECHSLER

EASY

Finished Felted Measurements

11 inches wide x 14½ inches deep
Measurements achieved using yarn and color specified; results may vary depending on yarn, yarn color and felting time.

Materials

- Plymouth Galway Worsted 100 percent wool medium weight yarn (210 yds/100g per ball): 4 balls each blue #15 (A) and ivory #1 (B)
- Plymouth Stars 50 percent rayon/50 percent nylon medium weight yarn (71 yds/50g per ball): 1 ball dark blue #150 (C)
- Size 13 (9mm) straight needles or size needed to obtain gauge
- Tapestry needle

Pre-Felted Gauge

12 sts and 16 rows = 4 inches/10cm with 2 strands A held tog
Exact gauge is not critical; make sure your sts are loose and airy.

Special Technique

I-cord: *K6, do not turn, sl sts back to LH needle; rep from * until cord is desired length. Bind off.

Pattern Notes

Hold 2 strands of yarn tog throughout.
On top edge, use tails from outside and inside ball of C to double it. This will ensure that you divide the yarn exactly in half.

This bag is worked using the intarsia method.

Each block is worked with a separate ball of yarn.

Make multiple small balls of 2 strands A, 2 strands B and 1 strand each A and B. When changing colors, bring the new color from under the old color to lock the sts and prevent holes.

The blocks are worked in multiples of 3. For a smaller purse, work 3 fewer blocks; for a larger purse, add 3 blocks.

Bag
Top Edge

With 2 strands A held tog, cast on 90 sts.
Join 2 strands C.
With 2 A and 2 C held tog, knit every row until C runs out.

Sides

Working in St st and using intarsia method, work according to the Chart. Each block of Chart is 10 sts wide and 20 rows high. Rep Chart 3 times across and 3 times up.
Bind off.
Weave in all ends.

Assembly

Sew side and bottom seams, matching corners of blocks.

Handles

With 2 strands A held tog, cast on 6 sts.
Work I-cord until it is approx twice the length desired.
Sew handle securely to inside of bag with each end starting just below the top edge.

Felting

Follow basic felting instructions on page 168 until finished measurements are obtained or bag is desired size.
Shape bag to dry. ✳

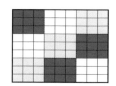

My Blue Checkerboard
Each block is 10 sts wide and 20 rows high

COLOR KEY
☐ 2 B held tog
■ 2 A held tog
☐ 1 A and 1 B held tog

Evening Envelope Clutch

THIS LITTLE CLUTCH IS PURE ELEGANCE. MAKE IT SPECIAL BY ATTACHING A VINTAGE BROOCH.

DESIGN BY SCARLET TAYLOR

BEGINNER

Finished Felted Measurements

7 inches wide x 4½ inches deep
Measurements achieved using yarns and colors specified; results may vary depending on yarn, yarn color and felting time.

Materials

- Plymouth Galway Worsted 100 percent wool medium weight yarn (210 yds/100g per ball): 1 ball red #16 (A)
- Plymouth 24K 82 percent nylon/18 percent lamé lightweight yarn (187 yds/50g per ball): 1 ball maroon #1373 (B)
- Size 13 (9mm) knitting needles or size needed to obtain gauge
- Tapestry needle
- Vintage (or new) brooch or pin

Pre-Felted Gauge

12 sts and 15 rows = 4 inches/10cm in St st
Exact gauge is not critical; make sure your sts are loose and airy.

Pattern Notes

Clutch front and back are constructed in 1 piece, then folded in half, with flap overlapping front piece, envelope style.
Hold 1 strand each of A and B tog throughout.

Purse

With 1 strand each of A and B held tog, cast on 26 sts.
Knit 4 rows.
Change to St st, beg with a RS row and work even until piece measures 16 inches from beg, ending with a RS row.

Shape Flap

Row 1 (WS): K3, purl to last 3 sts, k3.
Row 2 (RS): K3, k2tog, knit to last 5 sts, k2tog, k3. (24 sts)
Rep [Rows 1 and 2] 8 times. (8 sts)
Next row (WS): K2, k2tog twice, k2. (6 sts)
Next row: K1, k2tog twice, k1. (4 sts)
Next row: K1, k2tog, k1. (3 sts)

Bind off.
Weave in ends.

Assembly

Fold rectangular portion in half and sew side seams, leaving flap unsewn.

Felting

Follow basic felting instructions on page 168 until finished measurements are obtained or envelope is desired size.
Dry flat.

Finishing

Attach brooch or pin to flap as desired. ✳

Plenty of Pearls Clutch

WITH PEARLS AROUND YOUR NECK AND PEARLS ON YOUR BAG, YOU WILL BE SET FOR AN ELEGANT EVENING OUT.

DESIGN BY SCARLET TAYLOR

EASY

Finished Felted Measurements

9½ inches at top edge, 10 inches wide at bottom edge x 6 inches deep
Measurements achieved using yarns and colors specified; results may vary depending on yarn, yarn color and felting time.

Materials

- Plymouth Galway Worsted 100 percent wool medium weight yarn (210 yds/100g per ball): 1 ball each mulberry #141 (A) and ivory #1 (B)
- Plymouth Colorlash 100 percent polyester superfine weight knit-along yarn (220 yds/50g per ball): 1 ball magenta #215 (C)
- Size 10 (6mm) straight needles
- Size 11 (9mm) straight needles or size needed to obtain gauge
- Approx 63 [6mm] faux white pearl beads
- White cotton waste-yarn for stitch markers
- 1 large metal snap
- Sewing needle and white thread for sewing on beads
- Tapestry needle

Pre-Felted Gauge

16 sts and 15 rows = 4 inches/10cm in Block Check stitch with larger needles
Exact gauge is not critical; make sure your sts are loose and airy.

Special Abbreviations

Pm (place marker): Place marker on needle.
Sm (slip marker): Slip marker to other needle.
M1 (Make 1): Insert LH needle from front to back under the strand between the 2 needles; knit the strand tbl.

Pattern Stitch

Block Check (multiple of 6 sts)
See Chart.
[Work Rows 1–8] 4 times; [rep Rows 1–4] for pat.

Pattern Notes

Clutch front, back and side gussets are made in 1 piece, then joined at side.
Use short lengths of cotton yarn for st markers.
Beads are sewn on clutch after felting.

Clutch

Top Border

With smaller needles and holding 1 strand each of A and C tog, cast on 84 sts.
Knit 3 rows.
Cut C.

Divide Clutch

Next row (WS): Continue in garter st and k1 into the front and back of first st (1 st inc), pm between these 2 sts, k41, pm, M1, pm, k41, k1 into front and back of last st, pm

between these 2 sts. (87 sts)
Clutch is now divided as follows: 1 st for half of first side gusset, 42 sts for front, 1 st for 2nd side gusset, 42 sts for back, and 1 st for other half of first side gusset.
Set up pat: Change to larger needles and beg St st.
Next row (RS): Slipping markers as you come to them, k1 A, join B and work Block Check over next 42 sts, k44 A.
Work 9 rows even in Block Check and St st as established.

Shape Side Gussets

Next row (RS): K1, M1, sm, work Block Check to next marker, sm, k1, M1, sm, knit to last marker, sm, M1, k1. (90 sts)
Work 9 rows even in Block Check and St st.
Inc row (RS): K1, M1, k1, sm, work Block Check to next marker, sm, k1, M1, k1, M1, sm, knit to last marker, sm, k1, M1, k1. (94 sts)
Continue in pats as established, rep inc row every 10th row twice and *at the same time,* when Block Check has been completed, continue in St st and A only for 7 rows.
Clutch is now divided: 5 sts for half of first-side gusset, 42 sts for front, 8 sts for 2nd-side gusset, 42 sts for back, and 5 sts for other half of first-side gusset. (102 sts)

Assembly
Do not remove st markers.
Fold clutch in half width-wise, and
  join side seam at center of gusset.
Sew bind-off edges tog for bottom.
Weave in yarn ends.

Felting
Follow basic felting instructions
on page 168 until finished
measurements are obtained or bag
is desired size.
Shape to dry.

Finishing
Sew 1 pearl bead to each pink block.
Sew snap to inside top edges of
clutch. *

COLOR & STITCH KEY
■ With A, k on RS, p on WS
□ With B, k on RS, p on WS

6-st rep

Plenty of Pearls

Everyday Tote

THIS IS AN EASY-KNIT, EASY-CARRY BAG—IT'S JUST THE THING FOR EVERYDAY USE.

DESIGN BY SCARLET TAYLOR

EASY

Finished Felted Measurements

14½ inches wide x 8 inches deep
Measurements achieved using yarn and color specified; results may vary depending on yarn, yarn color and felting time.

Materials

- Plymouth Outback Mohair 70 percent mohair/26 percent wool/4 percent nylon bulky weight yarn (218 yds/100g per skein): 2 skeins blue variegated #854
- Size 11 (8mm) straight needles
- Size 13 (9mm) straight needles and circular needle or size needed to obtain gauge
- Stitch markers, 1 in contrasting color for beg of rnd
- Tapestry needle

Pre-Felted Gauge

10 sts and 13 rows = 4 inches/10cm in St st with larger needles
Exact gauge is not critical; make sure your sts are loose and airy.

Special Abbreviations

Pm (place marker): Place marker on needle.
Sm (slip marker): Slip marker to other needle.

Special Technique

3-needle bind off: Holding needles parallel with RS tog and WS facing, knit tog 1 st each from front and back needles, *knit tog 1 st each from front and back needles, then pass the first st over the 2nd to bind off; rep from * across.

Pattern Notes

The bottom of the bag is worked separately on straight needles (flat).
Sts are then picked up around bottom on circular needles and the bag is worked in the round until divided for front and back.

Bag

Bottom

With larger needles, cast on 21 sts.
Work in St st for 12 inches, ending with a WS row.

Body

Pick-up rnd (RS): With circular needle, k21, pm, pick up and knit 21 sts along long edge of bottom, pm, pick up and knit 21 sts along cast-on edge of bottom, pm, pick up and knit 21 sts along 2nd long edge, pm for beg of rnd and join. (84 sts)
Work even in St st and *at the same time,* inc 2 sts evenly across front and back of bag (4 sts increased) every 5th rnd 8 times. (116 sts)
Work even until bag body measures 15½ inches.

Divide for Front, Back & Straps

Next row: K10, turn.
Next row (WS): Bind off 4 sts, p54, turn.
Put rem 58 sts on holder for back.

Front

Continue working these sts back and forth in St st for front.
Next row (RS): Bind off 4 sts, knit across. (50 sts)
Work 5 rows even in St st.

Straps

*Next row (RS): K15, join a 2nd ball of yarn and bind off center 20 sts, k15.
Next row (WS): Working both sides at once with separate balls of yarn, k3, p9, k3.
Rep for 2nd strap.
Dec row (RS): First strap: knit to last 5 sts of first strap, k2tog, k3; 2nd strap: k3, k2tog, knit to end.
Maintaining first and last 3 sts of each strap in garter st, rep Dec row [every other row] 4 times, then [every 4th row] twice. (8 sts)
Work even until straps measure 8 inches from beg, ending with a WS row.
Place sts on holders.

Back

Sl back sts back to needle.
With RS facing, rejoin yarn and bind off 4 sts, knit to end of row.
Next row (WS): Bind off 4 sts, purl to end.
Work 4 rows even in St st.
Rep from * to shape straps same as for front.

Finishing
Join each front strap to a back strap
   by working a 3-needle bind off.
Sew short side seam where bag is
   divided.

Weave in loose yarn ends.

Felting
Follow basic felting instructions
   on page 168 until finished

measurements are obtained or bag
   is desired size.
Shape to dry. ✱

Elegant Evening Purse

THIS IS THE PERFECT LITTLE PURSE FOR THOSE SPECIAL OCCASIONS WHEN ALL YOU NEED TO CARRY ARE YOUR LIP GLOSS AND KEYS.

DESIGN BY SCARLET TAYLOR

EASY

Finished Felted Measurements

12 inches long at bottom edge, 8 inches long at top edge x 4½ inches deep

Measurements achieved using yarn and color specified; results may vary depending on yarn, yarn color and felting time.

Materials

- Plymouth Galway Worsted 100 percent wool medium weight yarn (210 yds/100g per ball): 2 balls black #9
- Size 13 (9mm) circular needle or size needed to obtain gauge
- Stitch markers
- Tapestry needle
- Beading stringing needle
- Approx 65 glass pebble beads #05161 from Mill Hill Beads/Wichelt Imports
- 2 (4½ inch x 5½ inch) black horseshoe-shaped purse handles
- Small metal snap
- Sharp sewing needle and thread to match yarn

Pre-Felted Gauge

14 sts and 16 rows = 4 inches/10cm in St st

Exact gauge is not critical; make sure your sts are loose and airy.

Special Abbreviations

B1 (Bead 1): Slide 1 bead up to needle.

M1 (Make 1): Insert LH needle under horizontal strand between stitch just worked and next st, k1-tbl.

Pattern Stitch

Slip-Stitch Bead (multiple of 4 sts + 3)

Row 1 (RS): K1, B1, *k3, B1; rep from * across row to last st, k1.

Rows 2 and 4 (WS): Purl.

Row 3: Knit.

Row 5: K2, *k1, B1, k2: rep from * across row to last st, k1.

Row 7: Knit.

Rows 6 and 8: Purl.

Rep Rows 1–8 for Slip-Stitch Bead pat.

Instructions for Slip-Stitch Beading

Knit to desired bead position (indicated in pat instructions by B1). Bring the yarn forward to the RS of your work between the 2 needles, and sl the next st (purlwise). Slide 1 bead up to the RH needle, placing it in front of the slipped st. Keeping bead in front of work, bring yarn back to WS, ready to knit.

Pattern Notes

Purse front, bottom and back are constructed in 1 piece, then

attached to side gussets.
Purse is beaded on front only.
A Chart is included for those
preferring to work beading pat
from a Chart.

Purse
Front
Using bead-stringing needle, pre-
string approx 60 beads.
Cast on 27 sts.
Knit 2 rows.
Work 4 rows of Slip-Stitch Bead pat.
Inc row (RS): K1, M1, work in pat as
established to last st, M1, k1. (29 sts)
Continue in pat as established, rep
inc row [every other row] 5 times,
then [every 4th row] twice, working
beads into pat as sts become
available. (43 sts)
Work even in pat until piece measures
approx 6¾ inches from beg, ending
with Row 1.
Place a marker at beg and end of
last row.
Discontinue working Slip-Stitch
Bead pat.

Bottom
Work even in St st for approx 4¾
inches, ending with a WS row.
Place a marker at beg and end of
last row.

Back
Work 4 rows in St st.
Dec row (RS): Ssk, knit to last 2 sts,
k2tog. (41 sts)
[Rep Dec row every 4th row] twice,
then [every other row] 5 times.
(27 sts)
Work 2 rows even in St st.
Knit 2 rows.
Bind off knit-wise.

Side Gusset
Make 2
Cast on 16 sts.
Work 6 rows in St st.
Dec row (RS): K1, ssk, knit to last 3
sts, k2tog, k1. (14 sts)
[Rep Dec row every 4th row] 3 times;
[rep Dec row every other row]
twice. (4 sts)
Purl 1 row.
Next row: K1, k2tog, k1. (3 sts)
Knit 2 rows.
Bind off knit-wise.

Assembly
Sew cast-on edge of each gusset
to side edge of bottom between
markers.
Fold front of purse up and sew side of
purse to side of gusset.
Rep for back.
Weave in all ends.

Felting
Follow basic felting instructions
on page 168 until finished
measurements are obtained or bag
is desired size.
Shape to dry.

Finishing
Sew 1 handle each to inside front
and back.
Sew snap to top-center inside of purse.
Sew on additional beads if necessary. ✱

STITCH KEY
☐ K on RS, p on WS
⦿ B1: Sl next st
purlwise wyif, slide 1
bead up to RH needle
in front of slipped st.
Keeping bead in front
of work, return yarn
to WS.

4-st rep

Elegant Evening

Victorian-Inspired Drawstring Bag

THIS BAG IS A THROWBACK TO SIMPLER TIMES—MAKE ONE
FOR EVENING USE, ANOTHER FOR YOUR LITTLE GIRL.

DESIGN BY SARA LOUISE HARPER

EASY

Sizes

Small (large) Instructions are given
for smaller size, with larger size in
parentheses. When only 1 number
is given, it applies to both sizes.

Finished Felted Measurements

7 (10½) inches wide by 5 (6½) inches
deep (opened up)
Measurements achieved using yarn
and color specified; results may
vary depending on yarn, yarn color
and felting time.

Materials

- Plymouth Galway Worsted
  100 percent wool medium
  weight yarn (210 yds/100g
  per ball): 1 ball gray #728
- Size 11 (8mm) 24-inch circular
  needle or size needed to obtain
  gauge
- 1-inch-wide stiff washable ribbon
  for felting
- 2 yds 1-inch-wide black satin
  ribbon
- 2 tasseled cords (25 inches long,
  including tassels) and matching
  cord embellishment (2-inch
  diameter)

Pre-Felted Gauge

14 sts and 16 rows = 4 inches/10cm
in St st
Exact gauge is not critical; make sure
your sts are loose and airy.

Bag

Cast on 25 (40) sts and work in St st
until piece measures 4 (8) inches.
Bind off all sts, then without cutting
yarn, pick up 15 (18) sts on the
shorter sides of rectangle and 22
(32) sts on longer sides. (74, 100 sts)
Join and place marker for beg of rnd.
Working circularly, knit all rnds until
piece measures 6 (9) inches.
Next rnd: *K2tog, yo; rep from * around.
Knit 4 more rnds, then bind off all sts.
Weave washable ribbon through
eyelets to avoid closure during felting.

Felting

Follow basic felting instructions
on page 168 until finished
measurements are obtained or bag
is desired size.
Shape to dry.

Finishing

Weave 2 satin ribbons for large bag,
or 2 cords for small bag, through
all eyelets in opposite directions.
Tie ends in an overhand knot.
Attach cord embellishment to small
bag. ✳

Shibori Bag

CARRY THE BEACH WITH YOU WHEREVER YOU GO. LITTLE POCKETS FORMED BY SHIBORI FELTING HOLD SHELLS (OR WHATEVER YOU WANT!), CREATING A TRULY UNIQUE BAG.

DESIGN BY JUDY RICE

INTERMEDIATE

Finished Felted Measurements

11 inches wide x 10 inches deep
Measurements achieved using yarn and color specified; results may vary depending on yarn, yarn color and felting time.

Materials

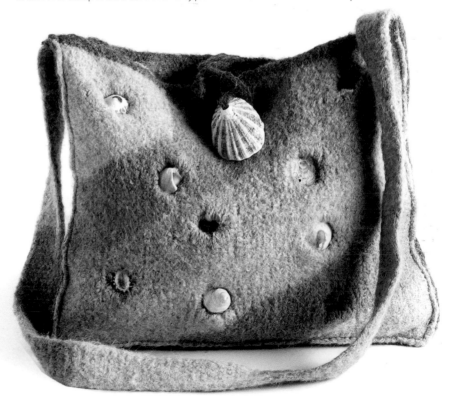

- Plymouth Suri Merino 55 percent suri alpaca/45 percent extra-fine merino medium weight wool (109 yds/50g per ball): 2 balls each light fawn #282 (A), medium fawn #208 (B) and light gray #401 (C); 1 ball dark gray #402 (D)
- Size 10 (6mm) straight needles or size needed to obtain gauge
- Bobbins (optional)
- Tapestry needle
- T-pins
- White cotton crochet thread or string (this must be sturdy)
- Assorted shells, approx 1 inch in diameter (see Pattern Notes)
- 1-inch-diameter mirror circles
- Plastic disks (1¼–1½ inches in diameter)
- Glue
- Sewing machine
- Large decorative shell button (optional)
- Waxed paper

Pre-Felted Gauge:

15 sts and 18 rows = 4 inches/10cm in St st

Exact gauge is not critical; make sure your sts are loose and airy.

Special Techniques

I-cord bind off: *K2, k2tog-tbl, do not turn. Sl 3 sts back to LH needle and rep from * across row until all sts are bound off. Bind off I-cord sts.

I-cord: *K4, do not turn, sl sts back to LH needle; rep from * until cord is desired length. Bind off.

Pattern Notes

Shibori is a Japanese term for a type of "resist", used in a lot of craft methods. In this Shibori bag, the twisted string and plastic pieces were used to "resist" felting and make little pockets.

This bag is worked using the intarsia method, working the colors with separate bobbins or lengths of each yarn. When changing colors, always pick new color up under the existing one.

The shibori pockets are formed in felting by tying plastic disks into the fabric. This will prevent the

fabric surrounding the disks from felting, resulting in stretchy pockets that indent to WS.

Cut plastic disks from firm plastic such as the lids from yogurt or cottage-cheese containers. The disks are cut to be approx the size of the object you want to glue on.

Examples of objects to be inserted are shells, sea glass, driftwood, and round mirrors. Do not pick heavy items like small rocks or items much larger than 1 inch.

Front & Back
Make 2

Cast on 18 sts with A, 18 sts with B, and 18 sts with C.

Row 1 (RS): K18 C, k18 B, k18 A.

Row 2: Join C. P1 C, p18 A, p18 B, p17 C.

Row 3: K16 C, k18 B, k18 A, k2 C.

Row 4: P3 C, p18 A, p18 B, p15 C.

Continue in this manner, shifting colors over 1 st each row and joining next color in sequence as on Row 2 when necessary, until colors are again 18 C, 18 B, 18 A. Stop shifting colors.

Work 18 C, 18 B, 18 A in vertical stripes for 4 inches, ending with a WS row.

Cut yarns, leaving 8-inch tails.

With D, cast on 3 sts to RH (empty) needle. Sl these sts to LH needle. Work I-cord bind off. Weave in all ends.

Strap

With D, cast on 10 sts.

Row 1 (RS): K8, bring yarn to front, sl 2 sts purlwise.

Rep Row 1 for approx 30 inches (115 garter ridges), ending with a WS row. Cut D.

Rep Row 1 for 23 garter ridges each in the following sequence: C, B, A, B, C.

Bind off.

Weave in all ends.

I-cord Loop Fastener (optional)

With D, cast on 4 sts and make I-cord

approx 12 inches long.

Prepare for Shibori Felting

Position plastic disks on RS of front and back pieces as desired; mark positions with pins.

Hold a disk in position on RS and turn fabric over; from WS, gather fabric around disk and tie a crochet cotton thread at top of gather to secure the disk in the "pocket" formed. Rep for all other disks.

Felting

Placing each piece (front, back, strap and I-cord) in separate mesh bags, follow basic felting instructions on page 168 until finished measurements are obtained or pieces are desired size.

This yarn felts very quickly, so check after 5 minutes, then every 2 minutes. Rinse in cool water and roll each piece in a towel to remove excess water. Snip the cotton string very carefully and remove disks.

Blocking

Shape front and back so that they are same rectangular size (shibori

treatment distorts the shape); pin on towels and dry flat.

Shape strap so that it has a consistent width of approx 1⅝ inches. Hang strap to dry.

Assembly

When pieces are thoroughly dry, sew tog as follows: With RS tog, pin 1 side of D-section of strap around 3 sides of back piece with vertical stripes at top. It is not necessary to fit D-section exactly to back piece; if necessary, cut excess D-section.

Pin other side of strap to front.

Use a machine, sew seam (seam will be on outside of bag).

Sew 2 ends of strap tog.

Finishing
Closure (optional)

Sew button to center front of bag.

Sew I-cord lp to center back of bag, cutting as necessary to fit.

Embellish

Put waxed paper inside bag (this will keep any glue leaks from gluing front and bag tog).

Glue desired objects into pockets. ✳

Commuter Lunch Bag

CARRY ANYTHING YOU WANT IN THIS GREAT, FELTED LUNCH BAG! WORKED CIRCULARLY, IT KNITS UP QUICKLY. THE TRICK TO THE "LUNCH BAG" LOOK IS ALL IN THE SHAPING.

DESIGN BY SARA LOUISE HARPER

EASY

Finished Felted Measurements

17 inches wide by 12 inches high (before sides are folded in)

8½ inches wide by 12 inches high (after sides are folded in)

Measurements achieved using yarn and color specified; results may vary depending on yarn, yarn color and felting time.

Materials

- Plymouth Outback Wool 100 percent wool medium weight yarn (370 yds/200g per skein): 2 skeins moss #901
- Size 10 (6mm) circular needle or size needed to obtain gauge
- Size 13 (9mm) double-pointed needles
- Tapestry needle

Gauge

16 sts and 19 rows = 4 inches/10cm in St st with smaller needles

Exact gauge is not critical; make sure your sts are loose and airy.

Special Technique

I-cord: *K6, do not turn, sl sts back to LH needle; rep from * until cord is desired length. Bind off.

Bag
Base

Cast on 43 sts and work back and forth in St st for approx 9 inches. Bind off all sts.

Sides

Pick up and knit 41 sts along longer sides and 37 sts along shorter sides. (156 sts)

Join and place marker for beg of rnd.

Rnd 1: *K38, p1; rep from * around (1 purl st in each of the 4 corners).

Work even for 21½ inches.

Bind off.

Handles
Make 2

Using 2 dpns, cast on 6 sts and work I-cord for 20 inches.

Attach handles to the wider sides of bag, 7 sts from edges and down 7 inches from top.

Felting

Follow basic felting instructions on page 168 until finished measurements are obtained or bag is desired size.

Shape into lunch bag form by creasing where the purl sts were worked. Fold base up and fold top over approx 3½ inches. Stuff and pin gently to keep shape during drying. ✳

Too-Cute Diaper Bag

BABY'S DIAPERS DESERVE A FESTIVE BAG. EMBELLISH THE BAG WITH I-CORD MOTIFS OF YOUR OWN CHOOSING.

DESIGN BY SCARLET TAYLOR

EASY

Finished Felted Measurements

15 inches wide x 10 inches deep
Measurements achieved using yarn and color specified; results may vary depending on yarn, yarn color and felting time.

Materials

- Plymouth Galway Worsted 100 percent wool medium weight yarn (210 yds/100g per ball): 3 balls mulberry #141 (A); 2 balls apricot #137 (B); 1 ball each of ivory #1, mint #111 and lavender #89
- Size 10 (6mm) straight needles
- Size 11 (8mm) straight needles or size needed to obtain gauge
- Embellish-Knit!™ I-cord maker (optional)
- Tapestry needle

Pre-Felted Gauge

13 sts and 17 rows = 4 inches/10cm in St st with larger needles
Exact gauge is not critical; make sure your sts are loose and airy.

Special Technique

I-cord: *K3, do not turn, sl sts back to LH needle; rep from * until cord is desired length. Bind off.

Pattern Note

Bag front, bottom and back are constructed in 1 piece (body), then attached to side pieces.

Diaper Bag
Body

With smaller needles and B, cast on 52 sts.
Knit 4 rows for top border. Cut B.
Change to larger needles and A.
Work even in St st until piece measures 40¾ inches from beg, ending with a RS row.
Change to smaller needles and B.
Knit 4 rows for top border.
Bind off loosely.

Sides
Make 2

With smaller needles and B, cast on 24 sts.
Knit 4 rows for top border. Cut B.
Change to larger needles and A.
Work even in St st until piece measures 17¼ inches from beg, ending with a WS row.
Bind off loosely.

Side Pockets
Make 2

With smaller needles and B, cast on 22 sts.

Knit 4 rows for top border. Cut B.

Change to larger needles and A.

Work even in St st until piece measures 8½ inches from beg, ending with a WS row.

Bind off loosely.

Front Pocket

With smaller needles and B, cast on 24 sts.

Work as for side pockets.

I-Cord
Appliqués

Using knitting needles or I-cord maker, make several 12-inch lengths of each ivory, mint and lavender.

Straps
Make 2

Using B, make 2 I-cords, each 3 yds long.

Assembly

Lay bag out evenly so that front and back each measures approx 17¼ inches and bottom measures approx 7 inches. Place markers on each side for bottom.

Sew bind-off edge of sides to side edges of bottom between markers.

Sew sides of front and back to sides, being careful to match borders at top edge.

Pin 1 side pocket to each side of bag at bottom edge and sew in place.

Center front pocket and pin to front of bag at bottom edge, sew in place.

Weave in yarn ends.

Felting

Follow basic felting instructions on page 168 until finished measurements are obtained or bag is desired size. Shape and stuff to dry.

Felt I-cords in a separate pillowcase or bag.

Finishing

Referring to photo, arrange I-cords into shapes as desired, cutting as necessary. Pin cord to bag as you shape appliqués. Baste, then sew in place, removing basting threads.

Whipstitch the 2 strap I-cords tog, making 1 double I-cord. Cut in half (1 strap for front and back).

Pin and baste front strap into place framing front pocket, with ends at bottom. Check for desired length and trim any excess if necessary. Sew in place, removing basting threads.

Rep for back strap, positioning it in alignment with front strap. ✳

Golden Mosaic Tote

THIS COMPLICATED-LOOKING COLOR PATTERN IS WORKED USING ONLY ONE COLOR AT A TIME—IT'S EASY!

DESIGN BY CINDY ADAMS

EASY

Finished Felted Measurements

14 inches wide x 9 inches deep
Measurements achieved using yarn
  and color specified; results may vary
  depending on yarn, yarn color and
  felting time.

Materials

- Plymouth Galway Worsted
  100 percent wool medium
  weight yarn (210 yds/100g per
  ball): 2 balls each gold #60 (A) and
  brown #66 (B)
- Size 13 (9mm) 24-inch circular
  needle or size needed to obtain
  gauge
- Tapestry needle

Pre-Felted Gauge

10 sts and 22 rows = 4 inches/10cm
  in Diamond Mosaic pattern with 2
  strands of yarn held tog
Exact gauge is not critical; make sure
  your sts are loose and airy.

Special Technique

I-cord: *K4, do not turn, sl sts back to
  LH needle; rep from *until cord is
  desired length. Bind off.

Pattern Stitch

Diamond Mosaic
Rnds 1 and 2: With B, *(sl 1, k1) 3
  times, sl 1, k3, (sl 1, k1) 3 times; rep
  from * around.
Rnds 3 and 4: With A, *K7, sl 1, k1, sl
  1, k6; rep from * around.

Rnds 5 and 6: With B, *(sl 1, k1) twice,
  sl 1, k7, (sl 1, k1) twice; rep from *
  around.
Rnds 7 and 8: With A, *k5, (sl 1, k1) 3
  times, sl 1, k4; rep from * around.
Rnds 9 and 10: With B, *sl 1, k1, sl
  1, k5, sl 1, k5, sl 1, k1; rep from *
  around.

Rnds 11 and 12: With A, *k3, sl 1, k1,
  sl 1, k5, sl 1, k1, sl 1, k2; rep from *
  around.
Rnds 13 and 14: With B, *sl 1, k5, sl 1,
  k3, sl 1, k5; rep from * around.
Rnds 15 and 16: With A, *k1, sl 1, k1,
  sl 1, k3, sl 1, k1, sl 1, k3, sl 1, k1, sl 1;
  rep from * around.

Rnds 17 and 18: Rep Rnd 13.
Rnds 19 and 20: Rep Rnd 11.
Rnds 21 and 22: Rep Rnd 9.
Rnds 23 and 24: Rep Rnd 7.
Rnds 25 and 26: Rep Rnd 5.
Rnds 27 and 28: Rep Rnd 3.
Rnds 29 and 30: Rep Rnd 1.
Rnds 31 and 32: With A, knit.
Rep Rnds 1–32 for pat.

Pattern Notes

This bag is worked with 2 strands held tog throughout.

Slip all sts as if to purl.

A Chart is included for those preferring to work mosaic pat from a Chart.

Since bag is worked in rnds, all rows on Chart are read from right to left. Each row is worked twice.

Knit the row with the color indicated after the row numbers and sl the sts in the opposite color.

Bag

Note: Bag is worked from top down.

With A, loosely cast on 128 sts.

Join without twisting, place marker between first and last st.

[Knit 1 rnd, purl 1 rnd] 3 times.

Buttonhole rnd: *K1, bind off 3 sts, k8, bind off 3, k7, bind off 3, k30, bind off 3, k6; rep from * once.

Purl the next rnd, casting on 3 sts over each set of 3 bound-off sts.

[Knit 1 rnd, purl 1 rnd] twice.

Work 32 rnds of Diamond Mosaic pat twice. Cut A.

With B, knit for 4 inches.

Loosely bind off all sts.

Assembly

Fold bag in half, with the 8 sts between bound-off buttonholes at each end.

With RS tog, sew bottom seam.

With RS tog, fold end corners into triangles and sew across bottom of mosaic pat.

Handle

Cast on 4 sts. Work I-cord for 80 inches.

Felting

Felt bag and handle in separate bags following basic felting instructions on page 168 until finished

measurements are obtained or bag is desired size.

Shape to dry.

Finishing

Weave handle through holes and tie ends tog with a square knot. ✳

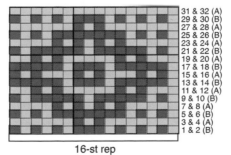

31 & 32 (A)
29 & 30 (B)
27 & 28 (A)
25 & 26 (B)
23 & 24 (A)
21 & 22 (B)
19 & 20 (A)
17 & 18 (B)
15 & 16 (A)
13 & 14 (B)
11 & 12 (A)
9 & 10 (B)
7 & 8 (A)
5 & 6 (B)
3 & 4 (A)
1 & 2 (B)

16-st rep

Golden Mosaic Tote

STITCH KEY
☐ On A rnd, k with A
  On B rnd, sl
■ On B rnd, k with B
  On A rnd, sl

Flying Geese Tote Bag

A WELL-KNOWN QUILT PATTERN TAKES FLIGHT ON A TOTE THAT IS SURE TO BECOME A FAVORITE.

DESIGN BY LOIS S. YOUNG

INTERMEDIATE

Finished Felted Measurements
Tote: 19 x 12½ x 3½ inches
Handles: 18 x 1½ inches
Measurements achieved using yarn and colors specified; results may vary depending on yarn, yarn color and felting time.

Materials
- Plymouth Galway Worsted 100 percent wool medium weight yarn (210 yds/100g per ball): 4 skeins red #44 (MC), 1 skein each light beige #138 (A) and black #9 (B)
- Size 9 (5.5mm) straight and double-pointed needles or size needed to obtain gauge
- Tapestry needle

Pre-Felted Gauge
15 sts and 20 rows = 4 inches/10cm in St st.
Exact gauge is not critical; make sure your sts are loose and airy.

Special Techniques
Attached I-Cord
With dpns and MC, cast on 3 sts. With WS of work facing you, *pick up and knit 1 st from top edge of tote, sl 4 sts to LH needle, k2, ssk, rep from * to end. Bind off.

I-Cord Seam
With dpns and MC, cast on 3 sts. With RS of work facing you and WS of 2 pieces held tog, *pick up and knit 1 st from back to front through both pieces, sl 4 sts back to LH needle, k2, ssk, rep from * to end of seam. Bind off rem I-cord sts.

Pattern Notes
Sl first st of each row purlwise wyif. On RS rows, move yarn to back between first and 2nd st to make chained selvage.
The Chart is worked using the intarsia method with separate lengths of yarn for each color. When switching from one color to the next, bring new yarn up from under previous yarn to lock sts and prevent holes.

Front & Back Center Panels
Make 2
With MC, cast on 32 sts.
Work 88 rows St st.
Bind off knitwise.

Front & Back Edge Panels
Make 4
With MC, cast on 13 sts.
Work 88 rows St st.
Bind off knitwise.

Side Panels
Make 2
With MC, cast on 13 sts.
Work 88 rows St st.
Bind off knitwise.

Bottom
With MC, cast on 76 sts.
Work 14 rows St st.

Bind off purlwise.

Pattern Panels
Make 4
Using A, cast on 11 sts.
Work Rows 1–8 of Chart 11 times.
Bind off in A.

Assembly
With A, and WS tog, sew pat panels to center and edge strips by overcasting loosely through chained selvages.
Work I-Cord Seam down each of 4 side seams, alternate picking up twice in 1 chained selvage st, then picking up once in next selvage st.
Attach bottom by working I-Cord Seam around bottom, working picking up once in each st, but picking up 3 times in each corner st. Sew end of I-cord to beg.
Work Attached I-Cord around top of tote, picking up once in each st and picking up 3 times in each corner st to match bottom. Sew end of I-cord to beg.
Weave in ends.

Handles
Make 2
Using MC, pick up and knit 11 sts centered along top of a pat panel behind I-cord border.
Next row: Sl 1, k10.
Rep previous row until handle measures 21 inches.
Bind off.

Sew handle securely behind I-cord, centered at top of pattern band on same side of tote.
Rep on other side of tote.
Weave in ends.

Felting

Follow basic felting instructions on page 168 until finished

measurements are obtained or tote is desired size.
Shape as necessary.
Dry flat. ✳

STITCH & COLOR KEY
- ☐ With A, k on RS, p on WS
- ☑ With A, sl 1 purlwise wyif
- ■ With B, k on RS, p on WS

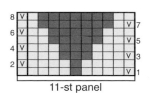

11-st panel

Flying Geese Tote

{ Neat Conveniences: Gifts & Things }

WHETHER LOOKING FOR A GIFT IDEA OR
SOMETHING TO ENHANCE YOUR STYLE,
YOU'LL FIND IT HERE.

On-the-Go Bottle Covers

KEEP YOUR WATER COOL AND YOUR BOTTLE DRY WITH THIS FELTED WATER-BOTTLE HOLDER.

DESIGN BY LAURA ANDERSSON & JUDY RICE

EASY

Sizes
Fits 16 (24) oz bottle. Instructions are given for smaller size, with larger size in parentheses. When only 1 number is given, it applies to both sizes.

Finished Felted Measurements
8½ (9½)-inch circumference x 6 (6¾) inches deep

Measurements achieved using yarn and colors specified; results may vary depending on yarn, yarn color and felting time.

Materials
- Plymouth Galway Worsted 100 percent wool medium weight yarn (210 yds/100g per ball): [16 oz size] 1 ball each in light sage green #121 (A), light green #127 (B), dark spring green #130 (C), black #9 (D); [24 oz size] 1 ball each light coral #136 (A), medium coral #107 (B), dark coral #148 (C), chocolate brown #66 (D)
- Size 10 (6mm) double-pointed needles or size needed to obtain gauge
- Size 11 (8mm) straight needles
- Stitch markers, 1 in contrasting color for beg of rnd
- Tapestry needle

4 MEDIUM

Pre-Felted Gauge
15 sts and 22 rows = 4 inches/10cm in St st using smaller needles

Exact gauge is not critical; make sure your sts are loose and airy.

Special Technique
I-cord: *K3, do not turn, sl sts back to LH needle; rep from * until cord is desired length. Bind off.

Pattern Stitch
Stripes & Dots
(even number of sts)

Rnd 1: With D, knit.
Rnd 2: With D, purl.
Rnd 3: With A (B, C), *k1, sl 1; rep from * around.
Rnd 4: With A (B, C), *p1, sl 1 wyib; rep from * around.
Rnds 5 and 6: Rep Rnds 1 and 2.
Rnds 7 and 8: With A (B, C), rep Rnds 1 and 2.
Rnds 9 and 10: With D, rep Rnds 3 and 4.
Rnds 11 and 12: Rep Rnds 7 and 8.

Rep these 12 rnds for pat, working A (B, C) in sequence as per instructions below.

Water-Bottle Holder
Sides
With smaller needles and A, cast on 40 (44) sts.

Distribute sts on 3 dpns and join without twisting; place marker between first and last sts.

Work in St st for 3 (4) inches.

Join D and work Stripes and Dots pat, alternating D and A. Cut A.

Join B and work Stripes and Dots pat, alternating D and B. Cut B.

Join C and work Stripes and Dots pat, alternating D and C. Cut D.

With C, work in St st for 1 (1¼) inch(es).

Next rnd (larger size only): *K9, k2tog; rep from * around. (40 sts)

Knit 1 rnd, placing markers every 8 sts.

Bottom

Dec rnd: *Knit to 2 sts before marker, k2tog; rep from * around. (35 sts)
Rep Dec rnd until 5 sts rem.
Cut yarn leaving 8-inch tail.
Using tapestry needle, thread tail through rem sts, and pull tight.
Weave in all ends.

Short (Long) I-Cord Strap

With larger needles and 1 strand each of C and D held tog, cast on 3 sts.
Work 30 (64) inches of I-cord.

Assembly

With tapestry needle and C, sew I-cord to each side of bag, beg at last rnd of pat section.
Weave in ends.

Felting

Follow basic felting instructions on page 168 until bag fits over 16 (24) oz bottle.
Allow the bag to dry on the bottle. ✳

Checkerboard Eyeglass Case

CARRY YOUR SUNGLASSES OR READING
GLASSES IN THIS QUICK-TO-KNIT FELTED CASE.

DESIGN BY CHRISTINE L. WALTER

Finished Felted Measurements
Approx 6 inches tall x 3¼ inches wide
Measurements achieved using yarn
    and colors specified; results may
    vary depending on yarn, yarn color
    and felting time.

Materials

- Plymouth Suri Merino 55
  percent suri alpaca/45
  percent extra-fine merino wool
  medium weight yarn (109 yds/
  50g per ball): 1 ball each of warm
  pink #1970 (A) and charcoal gray
  #402 (B)
- Size 10½ (6.5mm) double-pointed
  needles (set of 5) or size needed to
  obtain gauge
- Stitch marker
- Tapestry needle
- Decorative button

Pre-Felted Gauge
18 sts and 18 rows = 4 inches/10cm in
    Check st
Exact gauge is not critical; make sure
    your sts are loose and airy.

Pattern Stitches
A. Twined Knitting (even number of sts)
Rnd 1: Bring A and B forward to purl
and keep in front of work. *P1 B;
pick up A over B and p1 A; rep from

* around. Be sure to alternate colors
and bring next color over previous
color. Yarns will twist, but next rnd
will untwist them.
Rnd 2: With yarns still in front, * p1
B, pick up A under B and p1 A; rep
from * around. Again alternate
colors and bring next color from
under previous color. Yarns will
now untwist themselves.

B. Check Stitch (multiple of 6 sts)
Rnds 1–3: *K3 B, k3 A; rep from *
    around.
Rnds 4–6: *K3 A, k3 B; rep from *
    around.
Rep Rnds 1–6 for pat.

Eyeglasses Case
Base
With A, cast on 14 sts.
Knit 8 rows. Do not turn after last row.
With a 2nd dpn, pick up and knit 4
    sts along left side edge; with a 3rd
    dpn, pick up and knit 14 sts into
    cast-on edge; with a 4th dpn, pick
    up and knit 4 sts along right-side
    edge of base. (36 sts)
Redistribute sts evenly on 4 needles.
Join and place marker between first
    and last sts.

Sides
With A, knit 1 rnd. Join B.
Work 2 rnds of Twined Knitting.
[Work 6-rnd Check St pat] 3 times,

then work Rnds 1–3 once.
Work 2 rnds of Twined Knitting. Cut B.
With A, knit 1 rnd.

Edging
Turn work and cast on 3 sts using
    backward lp method.
Bind off loosely in I-cord as follows:
*P2, p2tog, sl 3 sts back to LH
    needle; rep from * until 7 sts rem
    on RI I needle.

I-Cord Button Lp
With a 3rd dpn, work unattached I-
    cord as follows:
*P3, sl 3 sts to back to LH needle; rep
    from * for 2 inches.
Continue I-cord bind off over last 7 sts.
Cut A, leaving an 8-inch tail.
Using Kitchener st, graft ends of I-
    cord edging.
With tapestry needle and A, sew
    button lp closed at edging.
Weave in ends.

Felting
Follow basic felting instructions
    on page 168 until finished
    measurements are obtained or case
    is desired size.
Dry flat.
If desired, reduce the fuzziness of
    the fabric by lightly shaving case
    using a disposable razor.
Sew button in place. ✳

Seat-Belt Cover

PROTECT YOUR NECK FROM AN ABRASIVE SEAT BELT BY WRAPPING THIS FELTED SEAT-BELT COVER AROUND IT.

DESIGN BY CINDY POLFER

BEGINNER

Finished Felted Measurements

Approx 6 x 10 inches
Measurements achieved using yarn and color specified; results may vary depending on yarn, yarn color and felting time.

Materials

- Plymouth Galway Worsted 100 percent wool medium weight yarn (210 yds/100g per ball): 1 ball mint #111
- Size 8 (5mm) straight needles
- Tapestry needle
- Sewing thread to match yarn
- Sewing machine or sharp sewing needle
- 12 x ¾ -inch piece of hook-and-loop tape

Pre-Felted Gauge

18 sts and 24 rows = 4 inches/10cm in St st
Exact gauge is not critical.

Seat-Belt Cover

Cast on 36 sts.
Work in St st for 14 inches.
Bind off.
Weave in ends.

Felting

Follow basic felting instructions on page 168 until finished measurements are obtained or piece is desired size.
Lay flat to dry.

Finishing

Using matching-color thread, sew the hook piece of tape to the long edge on 1 side of felted piece about ¼ inch from edge following diagram.
Sew the loop piece of tape to the other long edge on the opposite side of felted piece about ¼ inch from edge following diagram.
Fasten felted piece like a tube around seat-belt strap using the hook-and-loop tape. ✱

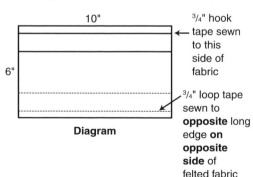

10"

6"

³/₄" hook tape sewn to this side of fabric

³/₄" loop tape sewn to **opposite** long edge **on opposite side** of felted fabric piece

Diagram

Car Organizer

KEEP CONVENIENCES AT HAND WITH A POCKET FOR A ROAD MAP AND LOOPS FOR YOUR COMPACT UMBRELLA.

DESIGN BY ELLEN EDWARDS DRECHSLER

INTERMEDIATE

Finished Felted Measurements

Organizer: 15 inches wide x 22 inches long (not including straps)

Straps: 6 inches long

Measurements achieved using yarn and colors specified; results may vary depending on yarn, yarn color and felting time.

Materials

- Plymouth Galway Worsted 100 percent wool medium weight yarn (210 yds/100g per ball): 5 balls turquoise #111 (A), 3 balls terra cotta #156 (B)
- Size 10½ (6.5mm) straight needles
- Size 13 (9mm) straight needles
- Cotton thread
- Button
- Tapestry needle

Pre-Felted Gauge

10 sts and 20 rows = 4 inches/10cm in garter st with larger needles and 2 strands held tog

Exact gauge is not critical; make sure your sts are loose and airy.

Pattern Notes

Organizer is worked holding 2 strands tog throughout except for top straps, which are worked with 1 strand.

The 5-st edges are worked in B using intarsia method. Use separate lengths of yarn for edges in each color and when switching from one color to the next, bring new yarn up from under previous yarn to lock sts and prevent holes.

Base

With larger needles and 2 strands B held tog, cast on 60 sts.

Knit 10 rows.

Next row (RS): K5 B, k50 A, k5 B.

Rep previous row until piece measures 30 inches from beg, ending with a WS row.

Dec row (RS): With B, k4, ssk; with A, knit to last 6 sts; with B, k2tog, k4.

Rep Dec row every other row until 18 sts rem, ending with a WS row.

With B, knit 10 rows.

Knit 8 sts and put on holder, bind off to last 8 sts, knit to end,

Left Strap

Cut 1 strand B and change to smaller needles.

With single strand B, knit 40 rows.

Buttonhole row: K2, bind off 4, k2.

Next row: K2, cast on 4 sts, k2.

Knit 8 rows.
Bind off.

Right Strap

Sl 8 sts from holder to smaller needle.
With smaller needles and single
  strand B, knit 50 rows.
Bind off.

Lower Right Pockets

First (larger) pocket

With larger needle and with 2 strands
  B held in back of work, pick up and
  knit 20 sts in the fabric, beg in 6th
  A garter ridge and 7th st from outer
  right edge.
Cut yarn, leaving tails to weave in
  later on WS.
Knit 1 row.
Inc row (RS): Knit in front and back
  of first 2 sts, knit to last 2 sts, knit in
  front and back of last 2 sts. (24 sts)
Knit 22 rows.
With A, knit 4 rows.
With B, knit 4 rows.
Bind off.

2nd (smaller) pocket

Skip 1 garter ridge.
With larger needle and 2 strands B,
  pick up and knit 20 sts directly
  above larger pocket.
Cut yarn, leaving tails to weave in
  later on WS.
Knit 1 row.
Work inc row. (24 sts)
Knit 4 rows.
With A, knit 4 rows.
With B, knit 4 rows.
Bind off.

Lower Left Pocket

With larger needle and 2 strands B,
  pick up and knit 20 sts in same
  ridge as first lower right pocket,
  beg in 7th st from outer left edge.
Knit 1 row.
Work Inc row. (24 sts)
Knit 38 rows
With A, knit 4 rows.

With B, knit 4 rows.
Bind off.

Center Large Pocket

Skip 3 garter ridges.
With larger needle and B, pick up and
  knit 48 sts, centering the pocket
  between outer 6 sts.
Knit 1 row.
Work Inc row. (52 sts)
Knit 20 rows.
With A, knit 4 rows.
With B, knit 4 rows.
Bind off.

Top Center Pocket

Skip 3 ridges.
With larger needle and B, pick up and
  knit 16 sts in fabric centered above
  large pocket.
Knit 1 row.
Work Inc row. (20 sts)
Knit 12 rows.
With A, knit 4 rows.
With B, knit 4 rows.
Bind off.

Umbrella Strap
Make 2

With larger needles and 2 strands B
  held tog, cast on 20 sts.
Knit 4 rows.
With A, knit 8 rows.
With B, knit 3 rows.
Bind off.

Assembly

Weave in all ends.
Loop umbrella straps and sew ends
  centered at bottom of each of the
  lower 2 pockets.
Sew pocket sides closed.
With B, sew center of large center
  pocket to fabric, creating 2 pockets
  from 1.
Baste pockets shut with cotton thread
  before felting.
Using tapestry needle, weave a
  length of B around outer edge
  of organizer drawing edges in
  slightly (this will keep edges

secure during felting process and
  prevent wavy edges).

Felting

Follow basic felting instructions
  on page 168 until finished
  measurements are obtained or
  organizer is desired size.
Shape and stuff pockets with small
  boxes or plastic bags.
Dry thoroughly.

Finishing

Sew button to top right strap,
  adjusting position based on car seat.

Twisted Strap

Cut 3 (4-yd) strands of B.
Tape 3 ends tog to a table or other
  unmovable object.
Twist strands until firm.
Without removing the tape, fold cord
  in half.
Remove tape and holding ends tog,
  let strands wrap around themselves
  to form twisted cord. Knot each end.
Sew cord to WS of organizer at lower
  edge of bottom pockets at point
  where B edging and A center meet. ✳

Felted Floral Accessories Bags

USE ONE TO HOLD YOUR BUSINESS CARDS AND THE OTHER TO CARRY YOUR COSMETIC NECESSITIES.

DESIGN BY CHRISTINE L. WALTER

EASY

Sizes
Small [to fit 3½ x 2-inch business cards] (large)

Finished Felted Measurements
Approx 4 (9) inches x 3¼ (8) inches
Measurement achieved using yarns and colors specified; results may vary depending on yarn, yarn color and felting time.

Materials
- Plymouth Outback Wool 100 percent wool medium weight yarn (370 yds/200g per skein): 1 skein of teal/aqua/purple mix #954 (MC)
- Plymouth Galway Worsted 100 percent wool medium weight yarn (210 yds/100g per ball): approx 50 yds each of yellow #137 (A), green #127 (B), coral #136 (C) and fuchsia #141 (D)
- Size 10½ (6.5mm) double-pointed needles or size needed to obtain gauge
- Stitch marker
- Tapestry needle
- Sharp sewing needle
- Thread to match MC
- 9-inch zipper for large bag
- Size 6/0 seed beads: 26 gold and 11 orange silver lined, or colors of your choice
- DMC metallic gold thread

Pre-Felted Gauge
16 sts and 22 rows = 4 inches/10cm in St st with MC
Exact gauge is not critical.

Special Techniques
3-Needle Bind Off
Hold the sts on 2 separate needles with RS tog.
With a 3rd needle, knit tog a st from the front needle with 1 from the back.
Rep, knitting a st from the front needle with 1 from the back needle once more.
Sl the first st over the 2nd.
Rep knitting a front and back pair of sts tog, then bind 1 pair off, until all sts are bound off.

Pattern Note
Flowers and leaves are cut from felted squares and sewn on as desired.

Model used a combination of back st and overcast st, with beads for embellishment.

Business Card Holder
With dpns and MC, cast on 34 sts.
Distribute on 3 or 4 dpns and join without twisting; place marker between first and last sts.
Rnd 1: Knit.
Rnd 2: Purl.
Rnd 3: Knit.
Rnd 4: Purl.
Rnds 5–14: Knit.
Sl sts evenly onto 2 dpns. (17 sts on each needle)
Turn bag inside out.
Close bag bottom using 3-needle bind-off.
Weave in ends.

Large Accessories Bag
With dpns and MC, cast on 76 sts.
Distribute on 3 or 4 dpns and join

without twisting; place marker between first and last sts.

Rnd 1: Purl.
Rnd 2: Knit.
Rnd 3: Purl.
Rnds 4–54: Knit.
Turn bag inside out.
Close bag bottom using 3-needle bind-off.
Weave in ends.

Flowers
Small squares
Make 1 each in A, B & C.
Cast on 24 sts.

Work in St st for 35 rows.
Bind off.
Weave in ends.

Medium square
With D, cast on 28 sts.
Work in St st for 42 rows.
Bind off.
Weave in ends.

Felting
Felt pieces separately following basic felting instructions on page 168

until finished measurements are obtained or bags are desired size.
Small square will measure approx 5 x 5½ inches; medium square will measure approx 5¾ x 6¼ inches.
Shape and dry flat.

Finishing
Using templates, cut flowers and leaves out of felted squares and sew to bag as desired.
Embellish with beads and embroidery if desired.
Sew zipper into large bag. ✱

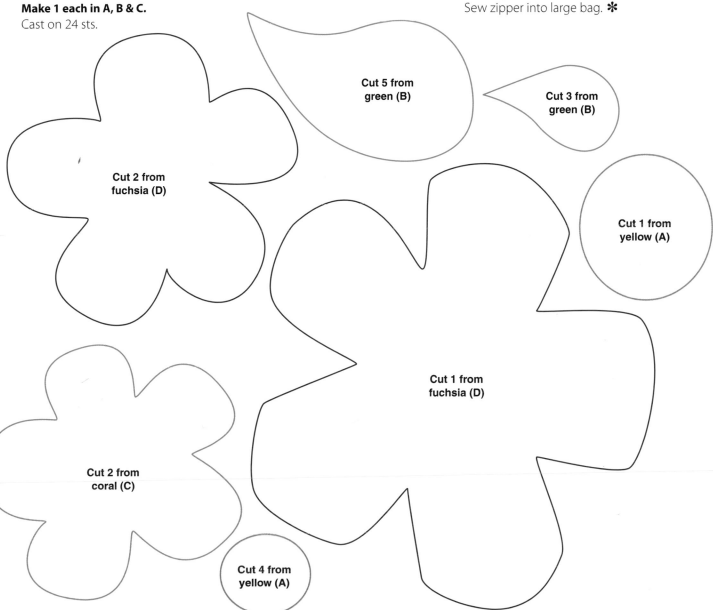

Cut 5 from green (B)

Cut 3 from green (B)

Cut 2 from fuchsia (D)

Cut 1 from yellow (A)

Cut 1 from fuchsia (D)

Cut 2 from coral (C)

Cut 4 from yellow (A)

Collection of Roses

A ROSE IS A ROSE, EVEN WHEN IT'S FELTED. THIS FLOWER WILL STAY FRESH ALL DAY (AND NIGHT) AND NEVER WILT.

DESIGN BY LAINIE HERING

BEGINNER

Sizes
Small (medium, large)

Finished Felted Measurements
Finished diameter of each size flower (and leaves) depends on the assembly and felting processes.

Materials
- [Small rose] Plymouth Baby Alpaca DK 100 percent baby alpaca light weight yarn (125 yds/50g per ball): 1 ball red #2060 (A) and green #5058 (B) **[3 LIGHT]**
- [Medium rose] Plymouth Alpaca Bouclé 90 percent alpaca/10 percent nylon super bulky weight yarn (70 yds/ 50g per ball): 1 ball each magenta #18 (A) and green #700 (B) **[6 SUPER BULKY]**
- [Large rose] Plymouth Baby Alpaca Grande 100 percent baby alpaca bulky weight yarn (110 yds/100g per skein): 1 skein each red #2050 (A) and green #3117 (B) **[5 BULKY]**
- Size 7 (4.5mm) straight needles [small rose]
- Size 10 (6mm) straight needle [medium rose]
- Size 10½ (6.5mm) straight needles [large rose]
- Tapestry needle
- Sharp sewing needle
- Matching thread
- Pin backs

Gauge
Exact gauge is not critical; make sure your sts are loose and airy.

Special Abbreviation
M1 (Make 1): Make a backward lp and place on RH needle.

Pattern Note
All roses and leaves are made from same instructions; use yarn and needle size indicated in materials list for size being worked.

Rose
With A and needles indicated for desired size, cast on 38 sts.
Row 1 (RS): Knit.
Rows 2, 4, 6, 8 and 10: Purl.
Row 3: *K2, M1, rep from * to last 2 sts, k2. (56 sts)
Row 5: *K3, M1, rep from * to last 2 sts, k2. (74 sts)
Row 7: *K4, M1, rep from * to last 2 sts, k2. (92 sts)
Row 9: *K5, M1, rep from * to last 2 sts, k2. (110 sts)
Bind off knitwise.

Leaves
Make 2
With B and needles indicated for desired size, cast on 3 sts.
Row 1 (RS): Knit in front and back of first st , k1, knit in front and back of last st. (5 sts)

Row 2 (and all even rows): Purl.
Row 3: K2, M1, k1, M1, k2. (7 sts)
Row 5: K3, M1, k1, M1, k3. (9 sts)
Row 7: K4, M1, k1, M1, k4. (11 sts)
Row 9: K5, M1, k1, M1, k5. (13 sts)
Row 11: Ssk, k9, k2tog. (11 sts)
Row 13: Ssk, k7, k2tog. (9 sts)
Row 15: Ssk, k5, k2tog. (7 sts)
Row 17: Ssk, k3, k2tog. (5 sts)
Row 19: Ssk, k1, k2tog. (3 sts)
Row 21: Sl 1, k2tog, psso. (1 st)
Fasten off and cut yarn.
Weave in ends.

Felting
Follow basic felting instructions on page 168 until pieces are desired size; st definition should no longer be visible.
Dry flat.

Assembly
Beg at one side edge of rose, begin a tight coil (spiral), sewing a few sts at base to close, as you go around.
***Note:** Rose can be made smaller at the start of this process by trimming off a portion of the piece, cutting parallel to this inner edge. The felting process protects this cut edge from fraying.*

Sew 2 leaves to rose, positioning as desired.
Sew pin-back to underside of rose. ✳

Fun-to-Wear Argyle Vest

TAKE THE CHILL OFF THE DAY WITH THIS ARGYLE INSPIRED FELTED VEST.

DESIGN BY CAROL MAY

INTERMEDIATE

Sizes
Woman's small (medium, large)
Instructions are given for smallest
size, with larger sizes in parentheses.
When only 1 number is given, it
applies to all sizes.

Finished Felted Measurements
Chest: 36¼ (43, 47¼) inches
Length: 20 (20¾, 21¾) inches
Measurements achieved using yarns
and colors specified; results may
vary depending on yarn, yarn color
and felting time.

Materials
- Plymouth Galway Worsted
  100 percent wool medium
  weight yarn (210 yds/100g
  per ball): 3 (4, 5) balls dark green
  #26 (A)
- Plymouth Imperiale Print 80
  percent super kid mohair/20
  percent nylon medium weight
  yarn (109 yds/25g per ball): 2 balls
  green/yellow/orange #4185 (B)
- Size 9 (5.5mm) 29-inch circular
  needle or size needed to obtain
  gauge
- 6 large bobbins
- Stitch markers
- Stitch holders
- Tapestry needle

Pre-Felted Gauge
18 sts and 24 rows = 4 inches/10cm
in St st

Exact gauge is not critical.

Pattern Notes
The charted diamonds are worked
with separate bobbins of B while
carrying A across entire vest.
The chart is worked in St st with each
row being worked twice.
The back neck shaping is created
by working the fronts longer than
the back; this throws the shoulder

seam to the back.
This vest is worked back and forth;
a circular needle is used to
accommodate the large number
of sts.

Body
With A, cast on 200 (236, 260) sts.
Set-up row (RS): K1 A, beg chart,
working rep indicated for size 6
times across, end k1 A.

Work in St st and maintaining first and last sts in A throughout, complete 54-row chart.

Next row (RS): Work Row 1 of chart, placing markers at sides as follows: k50 (59, 65), place marker, k100 (118, 130), place marker, k50 (59, 65).

Work Rows 2–4 of chart.

Next row (RS): K1 A, work chart over next 33 (39, 43) sts, knit with A only to last 34 (40, 44) sts, work chart, end k1 A.

Work even as established until piece measures approx 13 inches from beg, ending with a WS row.

Divide body & beg V-neck shaping

Next row: Maintaining pat as established, ssk,* work to 10 sts before marker, bind off 20 sts, rep from * once, work to last 2 sts, k2tog. (39, 48, 54 front sts rem; 80, 98, 110 back sts rem)

Work 1 row even on left front; sl right front and back sts to holders.

Left Front

Work 2 rows even.

Dec row (RS): Maintaining pat as established, ssk, work to last 2 sts, k2tog. (37, 46, 52 sts)

Rep Dec row [every 4th row] 2 (3, 4) times. (33, 38, 40 sts)

Dec at neck edge only [every 4th row] 13 (15, 16) times. (20, 23, 24 sts)

At the same time, when 2nd rep of chart is complete, work in St st with A only.

Work even until armhole measures 13 (14¼, 15½) inches, ending with a WS row.

Bind off loosely.

Right Front

Sl right front sts from holder to needle.

With WS facing, rejoin A.

Work 3 rows even.

Complete as for left front.

Back

Sl back sts from holder to needle.

With WS facing, rejoin A.

CONTINUED ON PAGE 129

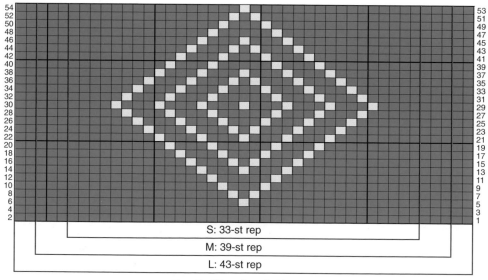

S: 33-st rep

M: 39-st rep

L: 43-st rep

Fun-To-Wear Argyle Vest

STITCH & COLOR KEY
■ With A, k on RS, p on WS
□ With B, k on RS, p on WS

Hold Your Needles

SLIP YOUR CIRCULAR NEEDLES INTO LABELED PLASTIC
BAGS AND KEEP THEM HANDY IN THIS NEEDLE CASE.

DESIGN BY ELLEN EDWARDS DRECHSLER

INTERMEDIATE

Finished Felted Measurements

7 x 4½ x 10 inches deep
Measurements achieved using yarn
and color specified; results may vary
depending on yarn, yarn color and
felting time.

Materials

- Plymouth Hand Paint Wool
  100 percent wool super
  bulky weight yarn (66
  yds/100g per skein): 6 skeins blue/
  turquoise #110
- Size 13 (9mm) straight needles
- Size 10½ (6.5mm) 29-inch circular
  needle or size needed to obtain
  gauge
- Large crochet hook
- Markers
- Tapestry needle
- Quart-sized plastic bags
- Shank button

Pre-Felted Gauge

8 sts and 11 rows = 4 inches/10cm in
garter st using larger needles
Exact gauge is not critical; make sure
your sts are loose and airy.

Needle Case
Front, bottom & back

With straight needles, cast on 30 sts.
Knit every row until piece measures
42 inches.
Bind off.

Place markers at each side 16 inches
from cast-on edge for front and
16 inches from bind-off edge for
back. The bottom is the 10 inches
between front and back.

Sides

Pick up and knit 20 sts along 1 side of
10-inch bottom.
Knit every row until side measures
same as front and back.

Bind off.
Rep on other side of bottom.
Sew sides to front and back.

Top edge

With circular needle, pick up and knit
18 sts along right-side edge, 20 sts
along front edge, 18 sts along left-
side edge, and 24 sts along back
edge. (80 sts)
Join and place marker between first
and last sts.

Knit 1 rnd, purl 1 rnd.
Bind off right-side, front and left-side
sts. (24 sts)

Flap
Change to larger (straight) needles.
Next row: K1 in front and back of first
3 sts, knit to last 3 sts, k1 in front
and back of last 3 sts. (30 sts)
Knit every row until flap measures
approx 14½ inches, ending with a
WS row.
Dec row (RS): K2tog, knit to last 2 sts,
k2tog.

Rep Dec row every other row until 5
sts rem.
Bind off.

Felting
Follow basic felting instructions
on page 168 until finished
measurements are obtained or case
is desired size.
Reshape case by stretching into a
square shape. Two clean bricks
wrapped in empty plastic bags
stacked 2 high makes a good
blocking form.

Allow to dry thoroughly.

Finishing
Crochet a chain long enough for a
loop that will fit around button.
Sew loop to outside end of flap.
Align and sew on button to front
of case.
If desired, make a pleat in each side of
case and sew tog at top edge.
Write needles sizes onto quart-sized
plastic bags with a permanent pen.
Place bags inside needle case. ✱

Fun-to-Wear Argyle Vest continued from page 126

Finishing
Weave in all ends.
Sew shoulder seams.

Felting
Follow basic felting instructions
on page 168 until finished

measurements are obtained or vest
is desired size.
If edges are wavy, continue to
felt edges by hand by rubbing
vigorously with soap and hot water
until they are straight.
Dry flat. ✱

Work 3 rows even.
Dec row (RS): Ssk, knit to last 2 sts,
k2tog. (78, 96, 108 sts)
Rep Dec row [every 4th row] 2 (3, 4)
times. (74, 90, 100 sts)
Work even until armhole measures
8 (8½, 9) inches, ending with a WS
row.
Bind off loosely.

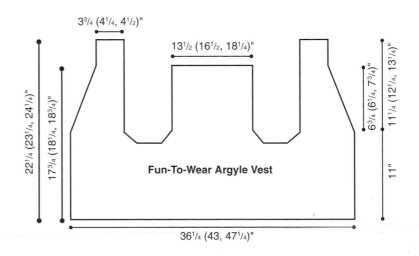

3³/₄ (4¹/₄, 4¹/₂)"

13¹/₂ (16¹/₂, 18¹/₄)"

22¹/₄ (23¹/₄, 24¹/₄)"

17³/₄ (18¹/₄, 18³/₄)"

6³/₄ (6¹/₄, 7³/₄)"

11¹/₄ (12¹/₄, 13¹/₄)"

11"

Fun-To-Wear Argyle Vest

36¹/₄ (43, 47¹/₄)"

{ Stylish Living: Vases, Pillows & More }

ADD THE WARMTH OF FELTED
ACCENTS TO YOUR SURROUNDINGS
WITH THESE INTERESTING PROJECTS.

Bobbled Vase & Flower

A FLOWER FOR THE TEACHER? THIS VASE AND FLOWER CAN STAY ON HER DESK THE WHOLE SCHOOL YEAR THROUGH.

DESIGN BY DONNA DRUCHUNAS

EASY

Finished Felted Measurements
Vase: 4 inch diameter x 10 inches tall
Flower stem: 17 inches long
Petals: 3½ inches long
Measurements achieved using yarn and colors specified; results may vary depending on yarn, yarn color and felting time.

Materials
- Plymouth Galway Worsted 100 percent wool medium weight yarn (210 yds/100g per ball): 2 balls medium blue #15 (A), 1 ball each light blue #143 (B), navy blue #10 (C), purple #13 (D) and green #82 (E)
- Size 15 (10mm) straight and double-pointed needles or size needed to obtain gauge
- Size 11 (8mm) double-pointed needles for flower
- Stitch markers, 1 in contrasting color for beg of rnd
- Tapestry needle
- Stitch holder
- 1 yard of ribbon (any kind)
- 18 inches of stiff floral wire, 26 gauge
- Wire cutters
- Fabric glue (optional)
- Sewing needle and thread to match flower color (optional)

Pre-Felted Gauge
9 sts and 12 rows = 4 inches/10cm in St st with larger needles and 2 strands held tog

Exact gauge is not critical; make sure your sts are loose and airy.

Special Abbreviation
Dec2 (decrease 2): Sl 2 sts tog as if to knit, k1, p2sso

Special Techniques
Bobble
Row 1 (RS): (K1, p1, k1, p1, k1) into the same st, turn. (5 sts)
Rows 2 and 4 (WS): P5, turn.
Row 3: K5, turn.
Row 5: Sl 2, k3tog, p2sso. (1 st)
Bobble complete.
I-Cord: *K5, do not turn, sl sts back to LH needle; rep from * until cord is desired length. Bind off.
Stripe Pattern (multiple of 5 sts + 5)
Rows 1 (RS) and 2: With C, knit.
Rows 3–6: With A, work in St st.
Row 7: With B, k3, make bobble, [k4, make bobble] to last st, k1.
Row 8: With B, purl.
Rows 9–12: With A, work in St st.
Rep Rows 1–12 for pat.

Pattern Notes
Vase is worked holding 2 strands tog throughout.
Flower is worked with a single strand of yarn.
Sides of vase are knit from bottom to top.

VASE
Sides
With larger needles and 2 strands C

held tog, cast on 40 sts.
Work Stripe Pat for approx 16 inches, ending after Row 6.

Top Border
With C, knit 6 rows.
Bind off.
Weave in ends.
Fold piece in half and sew side seam.

Bottom
With larger dpns and 2 strands A held tog, pick up and knit 40 sts around the bottom edge, placing markers every 10 sts.
Join and place marker between first and last sts.
Rnd 1: Knit.
Dec rnd: *Knit to 2 sts before marker, k2tog; rep from * around. (36 sts)
[Rep last 2 rnds] 3 times.
Rep Dec rnd until 12 sts rem.
Next rnd: K2tog around. (6 sts)
Cut yarn, leaving a 5-inch tail.
Using tapestry needle, thread tail through rem sts, and pull tight.
Weave in all ends.

FLOWER
Stem
With smaller dpns and E, cast on 5 sts.
Work 22 inches of I-cord.
Do not bind off.

Calyx
Row 1 (RS): Knit in the front and back of each st. (10 sts)
Row 2: Purl.

Row 3: *K1, knit in the front and back of the next st; rep from * across. (15 sts)

Cut E.

Row 4: Join D and purl.

Petals

Note: *Each petal of flower is worked back and forth over 3 sts. Put rem sts on holder or leave unworked on needle.*

Row 1 (RS): K1, yo, k1, yo, k1. (5 sts)
Row 2 and all even rows: Purl.
Row 3: K2, yo, k1, yo, k2. (7 sts)
Row 5: K3, yo, k1, yo, k3. (9 sts)
Row 7: K4, yo, k1, yo, k4. (11 sts)
Row 9: K5, yo, k1, yo, k5. (13 sts)
Rows 11 and 13: Knit.
Row 15: K5, dec2, k5. (11 sts)
Row 17: K4, dec2, k4. (9 sts)
Row 19: K3, dec2, k3. (7 sts)
Row 21: K2, dec2, k2. (5 sts)
Row 23: K1, dec2, k1. (3 sts)
Row 25: Dec2. (1 sts)

Fasten off.

Rep Rows 1–25 on each succeeding set of 3 sts until 5 petals have been worked.

Sew seam from stem to petals.

Sew bottom ¾ inch of each petal to the bottom ¾ inch of adjacent petal to form a flower.

Flower Center

With smaller dpns and B, pick up and knit 15 sts in the green purl bumps at the bottom of the petals on the inside of the calyx.

Knit 3 rnds.

Cut yarn, leaving an 8-inch tail.

Using tapestry needle, thread tail through rem sts, and pull tight.

Weave in all ends.

Use the tapestry needle to feed the ribbon up through the center of the flower stem and out through the flower center. Tie the ends of the ribbon tog so it does not come out during felting. This makes a channel inside the stem for you to insert the wire after felting.

Felting

Felt vase and flower separately following basic felting instructions on page 168 until finished measurements are obtained or pieces are desired size.

Fold the top edge of the vase to the outside like a cuff. Insert a drinking glass into the vase to shape it and allow it to dry thoroughly.

Finishing

While still damp, cut the ribbon and remove it from the stem.

Insert the floral wire into the stem in its place and clip off any excess wire with the wire cutters. Hang the flower upside down to dry thoroughly.

When dry, if desired, use sewing needle and thread to st the petals tog at the widest points to make a closed blossom. Put a dab of fabric glue on the openings at the bottom of the stem and the center of the calyx to secure the wire. ✱

Bows All Around Basket

THIS LOVELY FLUTED AND BERIBBONED BOWL
OFFERS CLEVER CLUTTER CONTROL.

DESIGN BY DONNA DRUCHUNAS

INTERMEDIATE

Finished Felted Measurements

7½ inch diameter x approx 3 inches tall
Measurements achieved using yarn
and colors specified; results may
vary depending on yarn, yarn color
and felting time.

Materials

- Plymouth Galway Worsted
  100 percent wool medium
  weight yarn (210 yds/100g
  per ball): 1 ball each burgundy #12
  (A), purple #132 (B) and pink #114 (C)
- Size 15 (10mm) double-pointed
  and 24-inch circular needles or size
  needed to obtain gauge
- Stitch markers, 1 in contrasting
  color for beg of rnd
- Size G/6 (4.25mm) crochet hook
- Tapestry needle

Pre-Felted Gauge

9 sts and 12 rows = 4 inches/10cm in
St st with 2 strands held tog
Exact gauge is not critical; make sure
your sts are loose and airy.

Pattern Stitch
(multiple of 10)
Rnd 1: *K1, yo, k3, sl 2 sts tog
knitwise, k1, p2sso, k3, yo; rep from
* around.

Rnd 2: Knit.
Rep Rnds 1 and 2 for pat, changing
colors as indicated in pat.

Pattern Notes

Bowl is worked holding 2 strands tog
throughout.
Rnd 1 of pat ends with a yo; make
sure this yo does not slip over the
beg of rnd marker.
Sides of bowl are knit from top to
bottom.
Change to dpns when sts no longer
fit comfortably on circular needle.

Sides

With circular needle and 2 strands A
held tog, cast on 70 sts.
Join without twisting; place marker
between first and last sts.
Knit 2 rnds.
Beg pattern st and at the same time,
work stripe sequence as follows:
With C, work 4 rnds.
With B, work 4 rnds.
With A, work 8 rnds. On last rnd, place
markers every 10 sts.

Shape Bottom

Continue stripe sequence and *at the
same time*, beg working bottom
decs as follows:
Rnd 1: Knit.

Dec rnd: *Knit to 2 sts before marker,
k2tog; rep from * around. (63 sts)
[Rep last 2 rnds] 3 times. (42 sts)
Work Dec rnd every rnd until 7
sts rem.
Cut yarn, leaving a 6-inch tail.
Using tapestry needle, thread tail
through rem sts, and pull tight.
Weave in all ends.

Felting

Follow basic felting instructions
on page 168 until finished
measurements are obtained or
bowl is desired size.
Put a small plate inside the bowl to
flatten the bottom and shape the
bowl into a circle. Dry thoroughly.

Finishing

With C, make 7 (21-inch-long)
crochet chains.
Use a tapestry needle to weave the
chains into the eyelet holes like
shoe laces. If you have trouble
getting the chains through the
holes, use the tip of a knitting
needle to open up the holes
before you weave in the chains.
Tie each chain into a bow.
If necessary, mist the bows with
water and form them into a
pleasing shape. ✳

Add a Holiday Accent

THIS RUFFLED BASKET IS JUST RIGHT FOR DISPLAYING BRIGHT BALLS OR COLLECTING HOLIDAY CARDS.

DESIGNS BY DONNA DRUCHUNAS

EASY

Finished Felted Measurements

Basket: Approx 7½ inches bottom diameter x 3 inches tall (excluding handles)

Candy Canes: Approx 7 inches tall
Measurements achieved using yarn and colors specified; results may vary depending on yarn, yarn color and felting time.

Materials

- Plymouth Galway Worsted 100 percent wool medium weight yarn (210 yds/ 100g per ball): 2 balls green #82 (A), 1 ball each white #8 (B) and red #16 (C)
- Size 15 (10mm) double-pointed and 24-inch circular needles or size needed to obtain gauge
- Size 11 (8mm) double-pointed needles for candy canes
- Stitch markers, 1 in contrasting color for beg of rnd
- Tapestry needle
- 2 yds of ribbon (any kind)
- 18 inches of stiff (26-gauge) floral wire
- Wire cutters
- Fabric glue (optional)

Pre-Felted Gauge

9 sts and 12 rows = 4 inches/10cm in St st with larger needles and 2 strands held tog
Exact gauge is not critical; make sure your sts are loose and airy.

Special Techniques

I-cord: *K4 (or 5), do not turn, slip sts back to LH needle; rep from * until cord is desired length. Bind off.

Pattern Notes

Basket is worked holding 2 strands tog throughout.
Sides of bowl are knit from top to bottom.
Change to dpns when sts no longer fit comfortably on circular needle.

BASKET
Brim Ruffle

With circular needle and 2 strands A held tog, cast on 135 sts.
Join without twisting; place marker between first and last sts.
Rnds 1 and 3: Knit.
Rnd 2: (K1, k2tog) around. (90 sts)
Rnd 4: (K1, k2tog) around. (60 sts)

Sides

Work even in St st for 6 inches.

On last rnd, place markers every 10 sts.

Bottom
Rnd 1: Knit.
Dec rnd: *Knit to 2 sts before marker, k2tog; rep from * around.
[Rep last 2 rnds] 3 times. (36 sts)
Rep Dec rnd until 18 sts rem.
Next rnd: K2tog around. (9 sts)
Cut yarn, leaving a 6-inch tail.
Using tapestry needle, thread tail through rem sts, and pull tight.
Weave in ends.

Braided Strap
Make 3 pieces
With larger dpns and 2 strands A held tog, cast on 4 sts.
Work I-cord for 24 inches.
Bind off.
Weave in ends.

CANDY CANES
Make 2 or as many as desired
With smaller dpns and a single strand of C, cast on 5 sts.
Work I-cord for 16 inches.
Change to B and work another 16 inches of I-cord.
Bind off.
Sew the 2 ends of the cord tog.
Weave in ends.

Use the tapestry needle to feed ribbon up through the center of the red section of I-cord. Tie the ends of the ribbon tog so it does not come out during felting. This makes a channel inside the candy cane for you to insert the wire after felting.

Felting
Felt basket and candy canes separately following basic felting instructions on page 168 until finished measurements are obtained or basket is desired size.
Put a salad plate inside the basket to flatten the bottom and shape into a circle.
Dry thoroughly.

Finishing
While still damp, cut the ribbon and remove it from the candy canes. Grasp the candy cane at both points where the red portion meets the white portion and pull on the ends to straighten it out. Insert the floral wire into the red portion of the candy cane in place of the ribbon and clip off any excess wire with the wire cutters.
Twist the candy cane several times to make the red and white sections wrap around each other, then bend

1 end over to form the candy-cane shape.
Dry thoroughly.
While still damp, braid the 3 strands for the strap and sew the ends tog so the braid doesn't come undone.
Dry thoroughly.
When dry, sew the straps to the inside of the basket. If you can't weave the ends into the felt, tuck them behind the straps and secure the ends with fabric glue. ✽

Bring in the New Year

**THIS GLITTERY, BEADED COZY AND COASTER SET
WILL MAKE ANY OCCASION FESTIVE. CHEERS!**

DESIGNS BY SCARLET TAYLOR

BEGINNER

Finished Felted Measurements

Cozy: 10½-inch circumference x 5 inches deep

Coasters: 4 inches square
Measurements achieved using yarns and colors specified; results may vary depending on yarn, yarn color and felting time.

Materials

- Plymouth Galway Worsted 100 percent wool medium weight yarn (210 yds/100g per ball): 1 ball ivory #1 (A) **4 MEDIUM**
- Plymouth Combolo 66 percent nylon/30 percent tactel/4 percent polyester bulky weight yarn (47 yds/50g per ball): 4 balls gold #1025 (B) **5 BULKY**
- Size 13 (9mm) straight needles or size needed to obtain gauge
- Stitch markers
- Tapestry needle
- Approx 48g Crystal Glass 6/0 E Bead Mix #67461 by Bead Heaven
- One package Designer Beads Mix #DJ10237-25 by Hirschberg Schutz & Co.
- Size 11 beading needle
- Beading thread to match yarn and beads

Pre-Felted Gauge

9 sts and 15 rows = 4 inches/10cm in St st with A and B held tog.
Exact gauge is not critical; make sure your sts are loose and airy.

Pattern Notes

Work with 1 strand each of A and B held tog throughout.
Beads are stitched to cozy and coasters after felting.

COZY
Sides

With 1 strand each of A and B held tog, cast on 32 sts.
Work in St st for 6 inches, ending with a WS row.

Bottom

Next row (RS): K3, k2tog, place marker, [k4, k2tog, place marker] 4 times, k3. (27 sts)
Next row and all WS rows: Purl.
Dec row: *Knit to 2 sts before marker, k2tog; rep from * across. (22 sts)
Rep last 2 rows until 7 sts rem, removing markers as necessary.
Cut yarn, leaving a 6-inch tail.
Using tapestry needle, thread tail through rem sts, and pull tight.
Weave in ends.
Fold piece in half and sew side and bottom seam.

COASTERS
Make 4

With 1 strand each of A and B held tog, loosely cast on 12 sts.
Work in St st for 5 inches, ending with a WS row.
Bind off loosely.
Weave in ends.

Felting

Felt cozy and coasters separately following basic felting instructions on page 168 until finished measurements are obtained or cozy and coasters are desired size (felt cozy a bit smaller than your bottle).

For a snug fit, stretch cozy over bottle to dry.
Dry coasters flat.

Finishing
Beading for Cozy

Thread beading needle and bring to inside (WS) of cozy; insert through upper edge to RS. Bring up needle, thread 2 (6/0 E) beads, then 1 Designer bead, then 2 (6/0 E) beads. Take needle back through bag to WS so that beads form a small lp.

Rep evenly around top edge.

Beading for Coasters

Thread beading needle. *Bring needle up through WS of one side edge of coaster, thread 3 (6/0 E) beads as desired (sample made with 1 gold bead in center of 1 each, white and crystal beads). Take needle down through RS edge of coaster in a slight diagonal line, then bring needle back up through WS in 1 motion. Rep from * evenly around all 4 edges of each coaster. ✳

Love Blooms Pillow

HEARTS AND LOVE GO TOGETHER ON THIS EASY-KNIT PILLOW—WHAT A HEARTWARMING PRESENT!

DESIGN BY GAYLE BUNN

BEGINNER

Finished Felted Measurements

Approx 14 inches square
Measurements achieved using yarn and colors specified; results may vary depending on yarn, yarn color and felting time.

Materials

- Plymouth Galway Worsted 100 percent wool medium weight yarn (210 yds/100g per ball): 2 balls each red #44 (A) and purple #13 (B); small amounts of black #9 (C), orange #91 (D) and ivory #1 (E)
- Size 8 (5mm) straight needles or size needed to obtain gauge
- Tapestry needle
- Wax pencil or tailor's chalk to mark templates.
- Sharp big sewing needle
- Thread to match yarns
- Pillow form, 14 inches square

Pre-Felted Gauge

20 sts and 26 rows = 4 inches/10cm in St st
Exact gauge is not critical.

Pattern Note

All pieces are knit in rectangles, then felted; shapes are cut from felted pieces.

Pillow Squares

Make 4 each with A & B
Cast on 45 sts.

Work in St st for 9 inches, ending with a WS.
Bind off.
Weave in ends.

Heart Square

With A, cast on 24 sts.
Work in St st for 5 inches, ending with a WS row.
Bind off.
Weave in ends.

Flower

Petal Piece

With D, cast on 24 sts.
Work in St st for 6½ inches, ending with a WS row.
Bind off.
Weave in ends.

Center

With E, cast on 12 sts.
Work in St st for 2 inches, ending with a WS row.

Bind off.
Weave in ends.

Felting

Using tapestry needle, weave a length of matching yarn around all outer edges of each pillow square drawing edges in slightly (this will keep edges secure during felting process and prevent wavy edges).

Follow basic felting instructions on page 168 until stitch definition is almost unrecognizable.

Dry flat.

Assembly

Cut each pillow square to measure 7 x 7 inches.

Using templates as guide and tailor's chalk or wax pencil, mark heart and 5 petals and center for flower on appropriate pieces of felt; cut out.

With C, work blanket st around outer edge of heart.

With E, work blanket st around outer edges of petals.

With D, work blanket st around outer edge of center.

Using photo as guide and tailor's chalk or wax pencil, mark "love" and "sweet" on purple pillow squares and embroider using E and outline st.

Assemble flower and sew to "sweet" square.

Sew heart to "love" square.

With C, work blanket st around outer edges of pillow squares.

Weave in and out of blanket st, joining squares to form front and back.

Sew 3 sides of pillow tog.

Insert pillow form.
Sew rem side to close. ✱

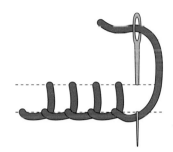

Blanket Stitch

Outline Stitch

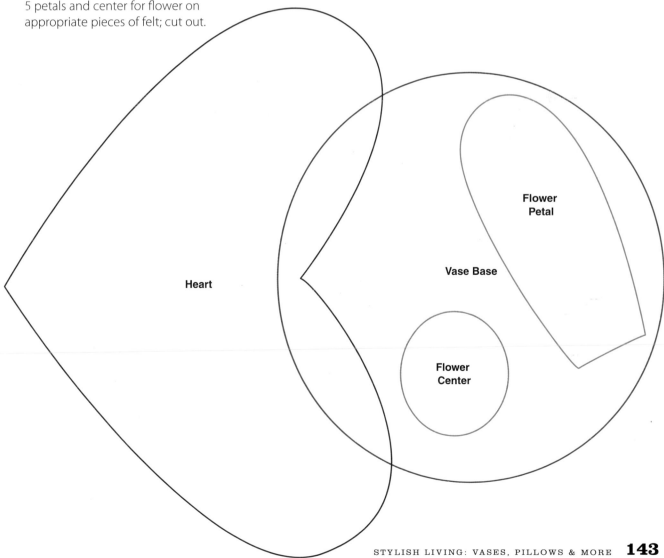

Heart

Vase Base

Flower Petal

Flower Center

Thoughts of Love Basket

WHY KEEP YOUR KNITTING PROJECTS IN A BAG? YOUR YARN WILL LOOK ESPECIALLY PRETTY SITTING IN THIS BASKET.

DESIGN BY GAYLE BUNN

EASY

Finished Felted Measurements

Approx 10½ inches in diameter x 5 inches tall (excluding handles)
Measurements achieved using yarn and colors specified; results may vary depending on yarn, yarn color and felting time.

Materials

- Plymouth Galway Worsted 100 percent wool medium weight yarn (210 yds/100g per ball): 2 balls red #44 (A), 1 ball purple #13 (B), and small amount black #9 (C)
- Size 10½ (6.5mm) double-pointed and 24-inch circular needles or size needed to obtain gauge
- Stitch markers, 1 in contrasting color for beg of rnd
- Tapestry needle

Pre-Felted Gauge

11 sts and 14 rows = 4 inches/10cm in St st using 2 strands yarn held tog
Exact gauge is not critical.

Pattern Notes

Basket is worked with 2 strands held tog throughout.
Change to dpns when sts no longer fit comfortably on circular needle.

Basket
Sides

With circular needle and 2 strands A held tog, cast on 96 sts.

Join without twisting; place marker between first and last sts.
Work 3 rnds in k2, p2 ribbing.
With B, knit 2 rnds.
With A, knit 4 rnds.
Rep last 6 rnds.
With B, knit 2 rnds.
With A, knit until piece measures 6½ inches from beg; on last rnd, place markers every 12 sts.

Bottom

Dec rnd: *Knit to 2 sts before marker, k2tog; rep from * around. (88 sts)
Knit 3 rnds.
Rep last 4 rnds. (80 sts)
Work Dec rnd on next, then [every other rnd] 4 times. (40 sts)
Work Dec rnd [every rnd] 4 times. (8 sts)

Cut yarn, leaving a 6-inch tail.
Using tapestry needle, thread tail through rem sts, and pull tight.
Weave in all ends.

Handles
Make 2

With dpns and 2 strands of A held tog, cast on 6 sts.
Distribute sts evenly on 3 dpns and join without twisting; place marker between first and last sts.
Knit around until piece measures 12 inches.
Bind off.

Felting

Felt following basic felting instructions on page 168 until

finished measurements are obtained or basket is desired size. Shape and stuff as necessary. Dry thoroughly.

Finishing

With C, work blanket st around top edge.

Sew handle ends to each side of basket approx 1½ inches below top edge. ✳

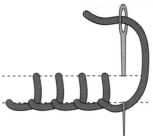

Blanket Stitch

Sweet Flower Vase

THESE EASY FELTED FLOWERS WILL ADD CHARM TO A BEDROOM OR OFFICE SPACE.

DESIGN BY GAYLE BUNN

EASY

Finished Felted Measurements

Approx 3 inches in diameter x
  5½ inches tall
Measurements achieved using yarn
  and colors specified; results may
  vary depending on yarn, yarn color
  and felting time.

Materials

- Plymouth Galway Worsted
  100 percent wool medium
  weight yarn (210 yds/100g
  per ball): 1 ball each red #44 (A) and
  purple #13 (B), small amounts black
  #9 (C), orange #91 (D), ivory #1 (E)
  and green #17 (F)
- Size 10½ (6.5mm) straight and
  double-pointed needles or size
  needed to obtain gauge
- Wax pencil or tailor's chalk to mark
  templates
- Sharp sewing needle
- Floral wire
- Size G/6 (4mm) crochet hook

Pre-Felted Gauge

11 sts and 14 rows = 4 inches/10cm in
  St st using 2 strands yarn held tog
Exact gauge is not critical.

Pattern Notes

Vase is worked with 2 strands held
  tog throughout.
**Templates referred to in this
  pattern are on page 143.**

Vase
Sides

With dpns and 2 strands of A held
  tog, cast on 28 sts.
Distribute on 3 or 4 dpns and join
  without twisting; place marker
  between first and last sts.
Work 3 rnds in k2, p2 ribbing.
With B, knit 2 rnds.
With A, knit until work measures 7
  inches from beg.
Bind off.
Weave in all ends.

Base

With 2 strands of A, cast on 17 sts.
Work in St st for 4 inches, ending with
  a WS row.
Bind off.
Weave in all ends.

Flowers
**Make 2 each using D and B for
  petal pieces and E and D for
  centers.**
Petal Piece

With 2 strands of yarn, cast on 24 sts.
Work in St st for 6½ inches, ending
  with a WS row.
Bind off.

Center Piece

Cast on 12 sts.
Work in St st for 2 inches, ending with
  a WS row.
Bind off.
Weave in all ends.

Felting

Felt pieces following basic felting
  instructions on page 168 until
  finished measurements are
  obtained.
Shape and stuff vase as necessary.
Dry thoroughly.

Finishing
Vase

With C, work blanket st around top
  and bottom edges.
Using templates on page 143 as
  guide and tailor's chalk or wax
  pencil, mark base and 5 petals
  and 2 centers for each flower on
  appropriate pieces of felt; cut out.
Sew base to bottom edge of vase.

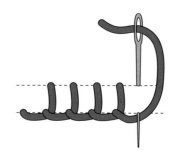

Blanket Stitch

Flowers

Using E for orange petals and D for
  purple petals, work blanket st
  around outer edges of petals.
Using D for ivory center and B for
  orange center, work blanket st
  around outer edge of centers.

Stems

Using 2 lengths of floral wire for each flower cover with F as follows:

Secure yarn at base of wire and using crochet hook, work sc around wire to cover.

Enclose end of wire between 2 flower centers and sew petals securely in place. ✳

Something Along the Edge

USE NEEDLE FELTING AND NOVELTY YARN TO ADD A SPECIAL DESIGN TO YOUR BOWL—MAKE IT AS INDIVIDUAL AS YOU ARE!

DESIGN BY DONNA DRUCHUNAS, NEEDLE-FELTING BY CAROL MANSFIELD

EASY

Size
Small (large) Instructions are given for smaller size with changes for larger size in parentheses. When only 1 number is given, it applies to both sizes.

Finished Felted Measurements
24 (29)-inch circumference
Measurement achieved using yarns and colors specified; results may vary depending on yarn, yarn color and felting time.

Materials
- Plymouth Outback Wool 100 percent wool medium weight yarn (370 yds/200g per skein): 1 skein blue/purple/turquoise multi #958 (A) **4 MEDIUM**
- Plymouth Outback Mohair 70 percent mohair/26 percent wool/4 percent nylon bulky weight yarn (218 yds/100g per skein): 1 skein blue/purple/turquoise multi #858 (B) **5 BULKY**
- Plymouth Athena 51 percent cotton/44 percent nylon/5 percent rayon bulky weight yarn (77 yds/50g per ball): 10 yds variegated #397 (C)
- Size 15 (10mm) double-pointed and 16-inch circular needles or size needed to obtain gauge
- Size G/6 (4.25mm) crochet hook (optional)
- Stitch markers, 1 in contrasting color for beg of rnd

- Tapestry needle
- Straight pins
- 36-gauge triangle needle-felting tool
- Foam rubber pad, about 10 inches square

Pre-Felted Gauge
9 sts and 12 rows = 4 inches/10cm in St st with 2 strands A held tog
Exact gauge is not critical. Make sure your sts are loose and airy.

Pattern Notes
Bowl is worked holding 2 strands of yarn tog throughout as indicated.
Change to dpns when sts no longer fit comfortably on circular needle.

The optional zigzag design on brim is needle-felted on after wet-felting the bowl.

Bowl
Brim
Using circular needle and 1 strand of A and B held tog, cast on 66 (76) sts.
Join without twisting; place marker between first and last sts.
Knit every rnd until brim measures 4 inches.
Purl 1 rnd (turning ridge).

Sides
Cut B and add a 2nd strand of A.
Next rnd: Dec 6 sts evenly around. (60, 70 sts)

Knit every rnd until sides measure 7 (8) inches from turning ridge.
On last rnd, place markers every 6 (7) sts.

Bottom

Dec rnd: *Knit to 2 sts before marker, k2tog; rep from * around. (50, 60 sts)
Rep Dec rnd every other rnd until 20 sts rem.
K2tog around until 4 sts rem.
Cut yarn, leaving a 5-inch tail.
Using tapestry needle, thread tail through rem sts, and pull tight.
Weave in all ends.

Felting

Follow basic felting instructions on page 168 until finished measurements are obtained or bowl is desired size.
Shape over a similar-sized bowl and dry.

Finishing

Crochet trim (optional)

Using a single strand of B, work 3 rnds of single crochet around the edge of the brim. If you have trouble pushing the crochet hook through the felted brim, use the tapestry needle to poke holes about ¼ inch apart around the entire brim and then make the crochet sts in these locations
Fasten off, weave in ends.

Needle-Felted Border (optional)

Mark brim with points of zigzag design about 2 inches apart using straight pins.
Tie very loose knots in novelty yarn C about 2 inches apart to match the points of zigzag design; twist yarn between knots.
Pin yarn in place with a pin in each knot.
Place brim on foam rubber pad and needle-felt several times along yarn to hold temporarily in place to make sure design fits around edge.
Pushing stray fibers into place while needle-felting, work around zigzag design until all fibers are well meshed.
Tuck end of yarn under the first point and needle-felt to secure. ✽

Diamond Mosaic Bolster

YOUR NECK OR LOWER BACK WILL THANK YOU FOR THIS COMFY PILLOW. THIS EASY TECHNIQUE USES ONE COLOR AT A TIME!

DESIGN BY CINDY ADAMS

INTERMEDIATE

Finished Felted Measurements

19-inch circumference x 27 inches long

Measurements achieved using yarns and colors specified; results may vary depending on yarn, yarn color and felting time.

Materials

- Plymouth Galway Worsted 100 percent wool medium weight yarn (210 yds/100g per ball): 2 balls navy #10 (A)
- Plymouth Outback Wool 100 percent wool medium weight yarn (370 yds/200g per skein): 1 ball teal #901 (B)
- Size 13 (9mm) 29-inch circular needle
- 4 feet ⅝-inch-wide ribbon
- Batting: 24 x 72 inches
- Tapestry needle
- Sewing thread and heavy needle

Pre-Felted Gauge

11 sts and 18 rows = 4 inches/10cm in mosaic pat

Exact gauge is not critical; make sure your sts are loose and airy.

Pattern Stitch

Diamond Mosaic (multiple of 16 sts + 3)

Row 1 (RS): With A, k1, *[sl 1, k1] 3 times, k3, [sl 1, k1] 3 times; rep from * to last 2 sts, sl 1, k1.

Row 2 and all WS rows: Using same color as previous row, knit the knit sts and sl the sl sts wyif.

Row 3: With B, k1, *k7, sl 1, k1, sl 1, k6; rep from * to last 2 sts, k2.

Row 5: With A, k1, *[sl 1, k1] twice, sl 1, k7, [sl 1, k1] twice; rep from * to last 2 sts, sl 1, k1.

Row 7: With B, k1, *k5, [sl 1, k1] 3 times, sl 1, k4; rep from * to last 2 sts, k2.

Row 9: With A, k1, *sl 1, k1, sl 1, k5, sl 1, k5, sl 1, k1; rep from * to last 2 sts, sl 1, k1.

Row 11: With B, k1, *k3, sl 1, k1, sl 1, k5, sl 1, k1, sl 1, k2; rep from * to last 2 sts, k2.

Row 13: With A, k1, *sl 1, k5, sl 1, k3, sl 1, k5; rep from * to last 2 sts, sl 1, k1.

Row 15: With B, k1, *k1, sl 1, k1, sl 1, k3, sl 1, k1, sl 1, k3, sl 1, k1, sl 1; rep from * to last 2 sts, k2.

Row 17: Rep Row 13.

Row 19: Rep Row 11.

Row 21: Rep Row 9.

Row 23: Rep Row 7.

Row 25: Rep Row 5.

Row 27: Rep Row 3.

Row 29: Rep Row 1.

Row 31: With B, knit.

Row 33: With A, knit.

Rows 35–68: Rep Rows 1–34, exchanging A and B.

Rep Rows 1–68 for pat.

Pattern Note

Pattern is worked back and forth in rows; a circular needle is used to accommodate the large number of sts.

Pillow

With A, cast on 99 sts.
Knit 10 rows.

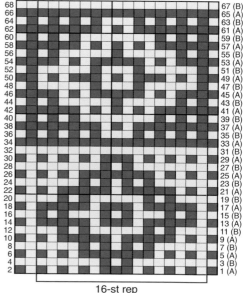

STITCH & COLOR KEY
- ■ On A row, k with A
  - On B row, sl with yarn to WS
- □ On B row, k with B
  - On A row, sl with yarn to WS

16-st rep

Diamond Mosaic Bolster

With B, knit 2 rows.
Beg chart and [work Rows 1–68]
   twice, then work Rows 1–32.
With A, knit 10 rows.
Bind off.
Weave in ends.
Sew side seam.

Felting

Follow basic felting instructions
   on page 168 until finished
   measurements are obtained or
   until pillow is desired size.
Shape and stuff with towels.
Allow to dry thoroughly.

Assembly

Roll batting and slide into pillow.
Cut ribbon in half (24 inches) and
   weave into fabric about ½ inch
   from navy border.
Pull to gather and tie in a square knot
   and then a bow. ✱

Love All Around Rug

"HUG" THAT SPECIAL LITTLE GIRL IN YOUR LIFE WITH THIS WARM HEART RUG!

DESIGN BY SARA LOUISE HARPER

INTERMEDIATE

Finished Felted Measurements

Approx 24 x 32 inches
Measurements achieved using yarn and colors specified; results may vary depending on yarn, yarn color and felting time.

Materials

- Plymouth Galway Chunky 100 percent wool bulky weight yarn (123 yds/100g per ball): 3 balls each red #16 (A) and purple #13 (B); 2 balls each pink #142 (C) and ivory #1 (D)
- Size 13 (9mm) 29-inch circular needle or size needed to obtain gauge
- Bobbins (optional)
- Tapestry needle

Pre-Felted Gauge

11 sts and 14 rows = 4 inches/10cm in St st
Exact gauge is not critical; make sure your sts are loose and airy.

Pattern Notes

The chart is worked using the intarsia method with separate lengths of yarn for each color. When switching from one color to the next, bring

COLOR KEY
- ■ Red (A)
- ■ Purple (B)
- ■ Pink (C)
- □ Ivory (D)

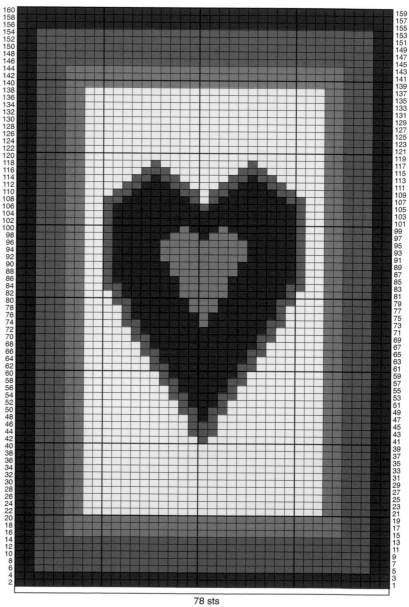

78 sts
Love All Around Rug
Each square represents 2 sts and 2 rows.
Work in St st throughout.

new yarn up from under previous yarn to lock sts and prevent holes. Each square on chart represents 2 sts and 2 rows.

Rug is worked back and forth in rows; a circular needle is used to accommodate the large number of sts.

Rug

With A, cast on 78 sts.
Work in St st following chart.
Bind off loosely.
Weave in all ends in similarly colored sections.

Felting

Using tapestry needle, weave a length of A yarn around outer edge of rug drawing edges in slightly (this will keep edges secure during felting process and prevent wavy edges).

Follow basic felting instructions on page 168 until finished measurements are obtained or rug is desired size.

Dry flat. ✱

A Vision of Love

THIS PRETTY PILLOW HAS TWO SIDES: THE "HEART" SIDE AND STRIPES ON THE REVERSE SIDE.

DESIGN BY SARA LOUISE HARPER

INTERMEDIATE

Finished Felted Measurements

Approx 14 inches square
Measurements achieved using yarn and colors specified; results may vary depending on yarn, yarn color and felting time.

Materials

- Plymouth Galway Chunky 100 percent wool bulky weight yarn (123 yds/100g per ball): 1 ball each red #16 (A) and purple #13 (B); 2 balls each pink #142 (C) and ivory #01 (D)
- Size 13 (9mm) 24-inch circular needle or size needed to obtain gauge
- Bobbins (optional)
- Medium-sized crochet hook
- Tapestry needle
- 3 heart-shaped buttons
- Sewing needle and thread

Pre-Felted Gauge

11 sts and 14 rows = 4 inches/10cm in St st.
Exact gauge is not critical; make sure your sts are loose and airy.

Pattern Notes

The chart is worked using the intarsia method with separate lengths of yarn for each color. When switching from one color to the next, bring new yarn up from under previous yarn to lock sts and prevent holes.
Each square on chart represents 2 sts and 2 rows.

Pillow is worked back-and-forth; a circular needle is used to accommodate the large number of sts.

Pillow

With C, cast on 46 sts.
Starting at center back and working in St st throughout, work stripe sequence as follows: *4 rows C, 4 rows D; rep from * until 44 rows are complete.
Work chart.
Work stripe sequence for 32 rows.
Work 2 rows C.
Bind off.
Weave in all ends in similarly colored sections.

Embellishment

With crochet hook and B, pull yarn from WS to RS, then chain a design directly under heart on the RS of fabric (see photo).

Felting

Follow basic felting instructions on page 168 until finished measurements are obtained or pillow piece is desired size.

Shape pillow if not completely rectangular; fold up the striped areas making sure they overlap. Dry flat.

Assembly

Fold lower striped section up, and with C or D, sew side seams.
Fold top striped section down, and with C or D, sew side seams to point of overlap with bottom section; leave rest of top unsewn.
Sew buttons along top of the striped area underneath the overlap, then carefully snip buttonholes in fabric just large enough to pull buttons through. ✱

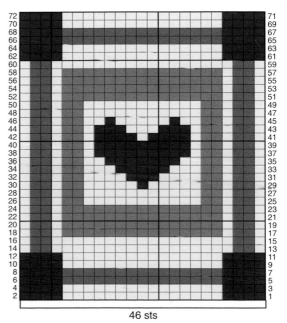

COLOR KEY
- ■ Red (A)
- ■ Purple (B)
- ▨ Pink (C)
- □ Ivory (D)

46 sts
A Vision of Love Pillow
Each square represents 2 sts and 2 rows.
Work in St st throughout.

Thick & Chunky Hot Pads

THESE COLORFUL HOT PADS/POT HOLDERS ARE QUICKLY KNITTED USING A VERY CHUNKY HAND-PAINTED WOOL.

DESIGN BY CINDY POLFER

■□□▭
BEGINNER

Felted Measurements

Approx 7–7½ inches square
Measurement achieved using yarn and colors specified; results may vary depending on yarn, yarn color and felting time.

Materials

- Plymouth Hand Paint Wool 100 percent wool super bulky weight yarn (66 yds/100g per skein): 1 skein desired color (Samples are shown in orange/ pink/brown #100, purple/red/ green #15, purple/blue/orange/ brown #201)

6 SUPER BULKY

- Size 15 (10mm) straight needles or size needed to obtain gauge
- Size K/10½ (6.5mm) crochet hook
- Tapestry needle

Pre-Felted Gauge

9 sts and 12 rows = 4 inches/10cm in St st
Exact gauge is not critical.

Hot Pad

With color of choice, cast on 19 sts.
Beg with a RS row, work in St st for 28 rows, ending with a WS row.
Bind off but do not fasten off last st.
Insert crochet hook in st lp and ch 9 sts.

Sl st to last bind-off st of pot holder to form a loop for hanging pot holder.
Fasten off, leaving a 3-inch tail.
Weave in ends.

Felting

Follow basic felting instructions on page 168 until finished measurements are obtained or hot pad is desired size.
Shape and dry flat. ✳

Come for Tea

THIS CHEERFUL TEA SET INCLUDES HOT PAD, COZY AND TEA BAG/SWEETENER HOLDER.

DESIGNS BY CHRISTINE L. WALTER

EASY

Finished Felted Measurements

Cozy: Approx 19-inch circumference x 10 inches tall (excluding loop)

Hot pad: Approx 7½ inches square

Tea holder: 15-inch circumference x 3½ inches tall

Measurements achieved using yarn and color specified; results may vary depending on yarn, yarn color and felting time.

Materials

- Plymouth Outback Wool 100 percent wool medium weight yarn (370 yds/200g per skein): 1 skein of fuchsia/aqua/orange/yellow #995
- Size 10½ (6.5mm) double-pointed and 24-inch circular needles or size needed to obtain gauge
- Tapestry needle

Pre-Felted Gauge

16 sts and 21 rows = 4 inches/10cm in St st

Exact gauge is not critical.

Special Abbreviation

Inc1 (increase 1): Knit in front and back of st.

Special Techniques

I-cord: *K3, do not turn. Sl 3 sts to LH needle; rep from *.

Attached I-cord: *K2, k2tog-tbl, sl 3 sts back to LH needle; rep from * around.

I-cord bind off: *K3, k2tog-tbl, do not turn. Sl sts back to LH needle and rep from * across row until all sts are bound off.

Purl I-cord bind off: *P3, p2tog, sl sts back to LH needle; rep from * until all the sts are bound off.

Pattern Notes

Tea Cozy is knit from the top down and is bound off using I-cord bind-off method.

Trivet is made using mitered squares, selvage sts, and attached I-cord around the edges.

Tea caddy is worked from the bottom up and also bound off using I-cord bind-off method.

TEA COZY

Cast on 4 sts.

Work I-cord for 3 inches.

Rnd 1: Inc1 in each st. (8 sts)

Distribute sts evenly on 3 or 4 dpns and join; place marker between first and last sts.

Rnd 2: Knit.

Rnd 3: Inc1 in each st. (16 sts)

Rnd 4: Knit.

Rnd 5: (K1, inc1) around. (24 sts)

Rnd 6: Knit.

Rnd 7: (K2, inc1) around. (32 sts)

Rnd 8: Knit.

Rnd 9: (K3, inc1) around. (40 sts)

Rnds 10 and 11: Knit.

Rnd 12: (K4, inc1) around. (48 sts)

Rnds 13 and 14: Knit.

Rnd 15: (K5, inc1) around. (56 sts)

Rnds 16 and 17: Knit.

Rnd 18: (K6, inc1) around. (64 sts)

Rnds 19–21: Knit.

Rnd 22: (K7, inc1) around. (72 sts)

Rnds 23–25: Knit.

Rnd 26: (K8, inc1) around. (80 sts)

Rnds 27–29: Knit.

Rnd 30: (K9, inc1) around. (88 sts)

Rnds 31–33: Knit.

Rnd 34: (K10, inc1) around. (96 sts)

Rnds 35–70: Knit.

Rnd 71: (K10, k2tog) around. (88 sts)

Rnds 72–74: Knit.

Rnd 75: Cast on 4 sts, turn.

Work purl I-cord bind off until all the sts are bound off; 4 I-cord sts will rem.

Graft 4 I-cord sts to cast on.

Sew I-cord at top of cozy to form loop. Weave in ends.

HOT PAD
First Square

Cast on 35 sts.

Row 1 (WS): K1-tbl, knit across.

Row 2 (RS): K1-tbl, k15, k3tog-tbl, k15, sl last st purlwise wyif.

Row 3: K1-tbl, knit to last st, sl last st purlwise wyif.

Rep last 2 rows, knitting 1 st fewer before center dec on each RS row, until 3 sts rem.

Next row (WS): K3tog.

Cut yarn and fasten off.

Second Square

With RS facing, pick up and knit 18 sts along cast-on edge, working from selvage to center dec. Turn work,

and using cable method, cast on 17 sts (35 sts).
Work in same manner as first square, beg with Row 1.

Third Square
Work in same manner as 2nd square, attaching 3rd square to 2nd square.

Last Square
With RS facing, pick up and knit 17 sts along cast-on edge of 3rd square, 1 st in center; and 17 sts along cast-on edge of first square. (35 sts)
Turn and work in same manner as first square, beg with Row 1.

I-Cord Bind-off Edging
With dpns, pick up sts along edge by inserting needle under selvage sts; do not knit them. Cast on 3 sts for I-cord.
*Work Attached I-cord to corner st, work 1 row unattached I-cord, work Attached I-cord in corner st; rep from * around.
Graft 3 rem I-cord sts to I-cord cast-on.
Weave in ends.

TEA HOLDER
Bottom
Cast on 14 sts.
Knit 42 rows.
Do not turn work after last row and do not bind off.
With dpns, pick up and knit 20 sts along left side of rectangle (1 st between each set of ridges), pick up and knit 14 sts along cast on edge, and pick up and knit 20 sts along right side of rectangle.
Join, placing marker between first and last sts.

Body
Work in St st for 24 rnds.
With RS facing, cast on 4 sts to LH needle.

Work I-cord bind off until all edge sts have been bound off; 4 I-cord sts rem.
Cut yarn leaving a 6-inch tail.
Graft last 4 sts to beg of I-cord.
Weave in ends.

Felting
Felt pieces separately following basic felting instructions on page 168 until finished measurements are obtained or pieces are desired size.
Note: *During felting process, remove tea cozy from washer once or twice and open the top lp by inserting your finger or a thick knitting needle to prevent it felting closed.*

Shape tea cozy by stretching over the intended teapot to dry.
Shape tea holder by placing a small box of tea wrapped in plastic inside and let dry.
Dry hot pad flat. ✳

Coasters & Covered Holder

PROTECT YOUR TABLE SURFACE WITH FELTED COASTERS THAT ARE ELEGANTLY STORED IN THEIR OWN LIDDED BOX.

DESIGNS BY CHRISTY PYLES

EASY

Finished Felted Measurements

Box: Approx 5-inch diameter
Lid: Approx 5¼-inch diameter
Coaster: Approx 4½-inch diameter
Measurements achieved using yarns and colors specified; results may vary depending on yarn, yarn color and felting time.

Materials

- Plymouth Outback Wool 100 percent wool medium weight yarn (370 yds/200g per skein): 1 skein purple/blue/tan #996 (A)
- Plymouth Outback Mohair 70 percent mohair/26 percent wool/4 percent nylon bulky weight yarn (220 yds/100g per skein): 1 skein purple/blue/tan #854(B)
- Plymouth Galway Worsted 100 percent wool medium weight yarn (210 yds/100g per ball): 1 ball each teal #139 (C), gold #60 (D) and purple #132 (E)
- Size 9 (5.5mm) double-pointed and 16-inch circular needles or size needed to obtain gauge
- Size 10½ (6.5mm) double-pointed and 16-inch circular needles
- Stitch markers, 1 in contrasting color for beg of rnd
- Tapestry needle

Pre-Felted Gauges

16 sts and 20 rnds = 4 inches/10cm in St st with smaller needles and A
12 sts and 15 rnds = 4 inches/10cm in St st with larger needles and 1 strand each A and B held tog
14 sts and 25 rows = 4 inches/10cm in garter st with smaller needles and 2 strands C, D or E held tog
Exact gauge is not critical.

Special Technique

I-cord: *K4, do not turn, sl sts back to LH needle; rep from * until cord is desired length. Bind off.

Pattern Notes

Lid and coasters are worked with 2 strands held tog as indicated.
Change to dpns when sts no longer fit comfortably on circular needle.
Coasters are worked using short rows to make "wedges."

BOX
Sides

With smaller circular needle and 1 strand A, cast on 70 sts.
Join without twisting; place marker between first and last sts.
Rnd 1: Knit.
Rnd 2: Purl.
[Rep Rnds 1 and 2] twice.
Work in St st until piece measures 5 inches from beg.

Bottom

Purl 2 rnds.
Knit 2 rnds and on 2nd rnd, place markers every 10 sts.

Rnd 1: *Knit to 2 sts before marker, k2tog; rep from * around. (63 sts)
Rnd 2: Knit around.
Rnd 3: *Knit to 2 sts before marker, ssk; rep from * around. (56 sts)
Rnd 4: Knit around.
Rep Rnds 1–4, then work Rnds 1–3. (28 sts)
Rep Rnd 1, then Rnd 3. (14 sts)
Next rnd: *K2tog; rep from * around. (7 sts)
Cut yarn, leaving an 8-inch tail.
Using tapestry needle, thread tail through rem sts twice, and pull tight.
Weave in ends.

LID

With larger circular needle and 1 strand each of A and B held tog, cast on 70 sts.
Join without twisting, place marker between first and last sts.
Rnd 1: Knit.
Rnd 2: Purl.
Rep Rnds 1 and 2.
Work in St st for 1 inch.
Purl 1 rnds.
Knit 2 rnds.
Dec as for bottom of box, beg with Rnd 1.
Weave in ends.

Handle

With larger dpn and A, cast on 4 sts, leaving a tail of at least 4 inches.
Work I-cord for 5 inches.
Bind off.
Using a tapestry needle, sew each

end of I-cord 2 inches from center of lid.
Weave in ends.

COASTERS

Make 2 each from C, D & E
With smaller needles and 2 strands held tog, cast on 7 sts.
Row 1 (RS): K7.
Row 2: K6, turn.
Row 3: K6.
Row 4: K5, turn.
Row 5: K5.
Row 6: K4, turn.

Row 7: K4.
Row 8: K3, turn.
Row 9: K3.
Row 10: K2, turn.
Row 11: K2.
Row 12: K1, turn.
Row 13: K1.
Row 14: K7.
[Rep Rows 1–14] 6 times. (Total of 7 wedges)
On 7th wedge, bind off on Row 14.
Sew cast-on and bound-off edges tog.
Weave in all ends.

Felting

Felt items separately following basic felting instructions on page 168 until finished measurements are obtained or pieces are desired sizes.
Shape box and lid, stuffing or using appropriately sized household containers as necessary (about 5-inch circumference) to aid in blocking.
Allow to dry thoroughly.
After completely dry, trim excess fuzziness carefully with scissors or razor to smooth surface appearance. ✳

Playtime Tic-Tac-Toe

THERE IS NO SIMPLER GAME THAN TIC-TAC-TOE, AND KNITTING THIS MAT IS JUST AS EASY!

DESIGN BY CAROL MAY

EASY

Finished Felted Measurements

25 x 28 inches
Measurements achieved using yarn
and colors specified; results may
vary depending on yarn, yarn color
and felting time.

Materials

- Plymouth Galway Worsted
  100 percent wool medium
  weight yarn (210 yds/100g per
  ball): 6 balls dark blue #10 (A), 2
  balls yellow #137 (B), 1 ball each
  green #130 (C) and orange #91 (D)
- Size 9 (5.5mm) 29-inch circular
  needle or size needed to obtain
  gauge
- 3 large bobbins
- Size H/8 (5mm) crochet hook
- Tapestry needle

Pre-Felted Gauge

18 sts and 24 rows = 4 inches/10cm
in St st
Exact gauge is not critical.

Pattern Stitch

Seed Stitch (odd number of sts)
Row 1: K1, *p1, k1; rep from * across.
Rep Row 1 for pat.

Pattern Notes

This pat is worked using the intarsia
method which uses separate
lengths of yarn for each color.

When switching from one color to
the next, bring new yarn up from
under previous yarn to lock sts and
prevent holes.
Before starting, wind 3 bobbins with B.
Pat is worked back and forth in
rows; a circular needle is used
to accommodate the large
number of sts.

GAME MAT

With A, loosely cast on 160 sts.
Purl 1 row.
Work in St st for 17 more rows, ending
with a WS row.
Next row (RS): K60 A, k5 B, k30 A, k5
B, k60 A.
Continue in St st in pat as established
for 79 more rows, ending with a
WS row.
Next row: K15 A, k130 B, k15 A.
Continue in St st in pat as established
for 7 more rows.
Next row: K60 A, k5 B, k30 A, k5 B,
k60 A.
Continue in St st in pat as established
for 33 more rows, ending with a
WS row.
With A, work in St st for 17 rows.
Bind off loosely.

Edging

With crochet hook and RS facing, beg
in any corner with A, work 1 rnd of
single crochet, working into every
other st on top and bottom and

every 3rd row on sides.
Work 1 rnd of reverse single crochet,
going in the opposite direction.
Fasten off and cut yarn.
Weave in all ends.
Using tapestry needle, weave a length
of A around outer edge of mat
drawing edges in slightly (this will
keep edges secure during felting
process and prevent wavy edges).

Playing Pieces

With C, cast on 17 sts.
Work in seed st until piece measures
at least 28 inches.
Bind off.
With D, cast on 17 sts and work as above.

Felting

Felt pieces separately following basic
felting instructions on page 168
until finished measurements are
obtained or mat is desired size and
playing pieces are at least the same
thickness as mat.
Shape as necessary; if edges are wavy,
continue to felt edges by hand by
rubbing vigorously with soap and
hot water until they are straight.
Dry flat.

Finishing

Cut 5 (3½-inch) squares from each
seed-st rectangle for playing pieces.
Cut small amount off each corner of
each square to make octagons. ✳

Checkers Anyone?

CHECKERS IS A GREAT ANYDAY PASTIME—PUT THE MAT WHEREVER AND START PLAYING!

DESIGN BY CAROL MAY

EASY

Finished Felted Measurements

Approx 32 inches square
Measurements achieved using yarn and colors specified; results may vary depending on yarn, yarn color and felting time.

Materials

- Plymouth Galway Worsted 100 percent wool medium weight yarn (210 yds/100g per ball): 6 balls each dark blue #10 (A) and red #16 (B)
- Size 9 (5.5mm) 29-inch circular needle or size needed to obtain gauge
- 8 large bobbins
- Size H/8 (5mm) crochet hook
- Tapestry needle

Pre-Felted Gauge

18 sts and 24 rows = 4 inches/10cm in St st
Exact gauge is not critical.

Pattern Stitch

Seed Stitch (odd number of sts)
Row 1: K1, *p1, k1; rep from * across.
Rep Row 1 for pat.

Pattern Notes

This pat is worked using the intarsia method with separate lengths of yarn for each color. When switching from one color to the next, bring new yarn up from under previous yarn to lock sts and prevent holes.
Before starting, wind 4 bobbins each with A and B.
Pat is worked back and forth in rows; a circular needle is used to accommodate the large number of sts.

Checkerboard Rug

With A, cast on 160 sts.
Purl 1 row. Cut A.
Row 1: *K20 B, k20 A; rep from * across.
Row 2: *P20 A, p20 B, rep from * across.
[Rep Rows 1 and 2] 17 times.
Next row: *K20 A, k20 B; rep from * across.
Continue working squares as established for total of 36 rows.
Continue alternating squares every 36 rows until 8 rows of squares are completed.
With A, purl 1 row.
Bind off loosely with A.

Edging

With crochet hook and RS facing, beg in any corner with A, work 1 rnd of single crochet, working into every other st on top and bottom and every 3rd row on sides.
Work 1 rnd of reverse single crochet, going in the opposite direction. Cut yarn.
Using tapestry needle, weave a length of A around outer edge of rug drawing edges in slightly (this will keep edges secure during felting process and prevent wavy edges).

Playing Pieces

With A, cast on 61 sts.
Work in seed st until piece measures at least 18 inches.
Bind off loosely
With B, cast on 61 sts and work as above.

Felting

Felt pieces separately following basic felting instructions on page 168 until finished measurements are obtained or rug is desired size and playing pieces are at least the same thickness as rug.
Shape as necessary; if edges are wavy, continue to felt edges by hand by rubbing vigorously with soap and hot water until they are straight.
Dry flat.

Finishing

Cut 12 (3½-inch-diameter) circles from each seed-st rectangle for playing pieces. ✸

Backgammon Rug

THIS RUG IS AN ATTRACTIVE ROOM ACCENT EVEN WHEN NOT BEING USED FOR A GAME.

DESIGN BY CAROL MAY

INTERMEDIATE

Finished Felted Measurements

48 x 50 inches

Measurements achieved using yarn and colors specified; results may vary depending on yarn, yarn color and felting time.

Materials

- Plymouth Galway Worsted 100 percent wool medium weight yarn (210 yds/100g per ball): 6 balls dark teal #131 (A), 3 balls each terra cotta #156 (B) and beige #138 (C)
- Size 9 (5.5mm) 29-inch circular needle
- Large bobbins (optional)
- Size H/8 (5mm) crochet hook
- Tapestry needle

Pre-Felted Gauge

4½ sts and 24 rows = 4 inches/10cm in St st

Exact gauge is not critical.

Pattern Stitches

A. Seed Stitch (odd number of sts)

Row 1: K1, *p1, k1; rep from * across.

Rep Row 1 for pat.

B. Wedges

Row 1 (RS): K5 B, k205 A, k5 C.

Row 2: P12 C, p191 A, p12 B.

Row 3: K19 B, k177 A, k19 C.

Row 4: P26 C, p163 A, p26 B.

Row 5: K33 B, 149 A, k33 C.

Row 6: P40 C, p135 A, p40 B.

Row 7: K47 B, k121 A, k47 C.

Row 8: P54 C, p107 A, p54 B.

Row 9: K61 B, k93 A, k61 C.

Row 10: P68 C, p79 A, p68 B.

Row 11: K75 B, k65 A, k75 C.

Row 12: P82 C, p51 A, p82 B.

Row 13: K89 B, k37 A, k89 C.

Row 14: P89 C, p37 A, p89 B.

Row 15: K82 B, k51 A, k82 C.

Row 16: P75 C, k65 A, p75 B.

Row 17: K68 B, k79 A, k68 C.

Row 18: P61 C, k93 A, p61 B.

Row 19: K54 B, k107 A, k54 C.

Row 20: P47 C, p121 A, p47 B.

Row 21: K40 B, k135 A, k40 C.

Row 22: P33 C, p149 A, p33 B.

Row 23: K26 B, k163 A, k26 C.

Row 24: P19 C, p177 A, p19 B.

Row 25: K12 B, k191 A, k12 C.

Row 26: P5 C, k205 A, p4 B.

Rows 27–52: Work as for Rows 1–26, but switch B and C with each other.

Rep Rows 1–52 for pat.

Pattern Notes

This pat is worked using the intarsia method which uses separate lengths of yarn for each color. When switching from one color to the next, bring new yarn up from under previous yarn to lock sts and prevent holes.

Pat is worked back and forth in rows; a circular needle is used to accommodate the large number of sts.

Backgammon Rug

First Side

With A, cast on 215 sts.

Work 2 rows St st.

Work 3 reps of 52-row Wedge pat.

Work 2 rows St st.

Center Bar

Row 1: With A, work seed st across.

Row 2: With B, work seed st across.

[Rep Rows 1 and 2] 11 times.

2nd Side

Work as for first side.

Bind off loosely.

Weave in all ends.

Edging

With crochet hook and RS facing, beg in any corner with A, work 1 rnd of single crochet, working into every other st on top and bottom, and every 3rd row on sides.

Work 1 rnd of reverse single crochet, going in the opposite direction.

Fasten off and cut yarn.

Weave in all ends.

Using tapestry needle, weave a length of A around outer edge of rug drawing edges in slightly (this will keep edges secure during felting process and prevent wavy edges).

Playing Pieces

With B, cast on 61 sts.

Work in seed st until piece measures at least 20 inches.

Bind off loosely.

With C, cast on 61 sts and work in seed as above.

Felting

Felt mat and colored rectangles separately following basic felting instructions on page 168 until finished measurements are obtained or mat is desired size.

If edges are wavy, continue to felt them by hand by rubbing vigorously with soap and hot water until they are straight. Dry flat.

Finishing

Cut 15 (2½-inch) circles from each colored rectangle for playing pieces. ✳

Felting Instructions

The Felt Formula

Felting is not a precise science. Wool felts when exposed to water, heat, agitation and change in temperature (hot-to-cold), but each element is hard to control precisely. As a result, each individual project may vary in the way it felts.

Technically, felting is the term used when one creates felted fabric from wool roving. (Roving is unspun wool.) Creating felted fabric from knitted (or crocheted) wool yarn is called fulling. Today the term felting is commonly used to describe both processes.

Felting can be done in the sink but goes much more quickly in a washing machine. Each washing machine is different, and the amount your machine felts a piece after one cycle may vary from your neighbors'. So be sure to follow the specific felting instructions for the piece you are making and check your piece several times during the felting process to make sure you are getting the desired results.

The felting process releases fibers which can clog your washing machine. Therefore, you may want to place items to be felted in a roomy mesh bag or a zipped pillowcase before putting them in the washing machine. Also, adding other laundry (such as jeans) when felting will increase the amount of agitation and speed up the process. Items such as towels are not recommended as they shed fibers of their own that can cling to the piece.

Felting Facts

Felting a knit or crochet piece made from wool makes it shrink. Therefore, the piece you knit must be much larger than the desired finished felted size. Fabric knit at a very loose gauge will shrink more than that knit at a more standard gauge.

Shrinkage varies since there are so many factors that affect it. These variables include water temperature, the hardness of the water, how much (and how long) the piece is agitated, the amount and type of soap used, yarn brand, fiber content and color. Felting works best on wool, alpaca and mohair that has not been preshrunk or treated to resist shrinking.

You can control how much your piece felts by watching it closely. Check your piece after about 10 minutes to see how quickly it is felting. Look at the stitch definition and size to determine if the piece has been felted enough. This is easier to achieve with a top-loading washing machine. Front-loading machines lock during the wash cycle and can not be opened mid-cycle for purposes of checking the piece. Small pieces may be felted by hand in a sink or washtub.

How to Felt

Place items to be felted in the washing machine along with one tablespoon of dish soap and a pair of jeans or other laundry. (Remember, do not wash felting with other clothing that releases its own fibers, or you will have these fibers in your project.) Set washing machine on smallest load using hot water. Start the machine and check the progress after ten minutes. Check progress more frequently after piece starts to felt. Reset the machine, if needed, to continue the agitation cycle. Do not allow machine to drain and spin until the piece is the desired size; creases can form in the fabric during the rapid spin cycle. As the piece becomes more felted, you may need to pull it into shape. When the piece has felted to the desired size, rinse it by hand in warm water—a cold-water rinse will continue the felting process. Remove the excess water either by rolling item in a towel and squeezing, or in the spin cycle of your washing machine.

Block the piece into shape, and let air-dry. Do not dry in clothes dryer. For projects that need to conform to a particular shape (such as a hat or purse), stuff the piece with a towel to help it hold its shape while drying. Household items like bowls make good blocking forms. Felted items are very strong, so don't be afraid to push and pull it into the desired shape. It may take several hours or several days for the piece to dry completely.

After the piece is completely dry, excess fuzziness can be trimmed with scissors if a smoother surface is desired—or the piece can be brushed for a fuzzier appearance.

Reducing Wavy Edges

The edges of large pieces of fabric often felt more slowly than the center of the fabric which results in wavy edges. One method of reducing wavy edges is to use a tapestry needle to weave a length of matching yarn through the

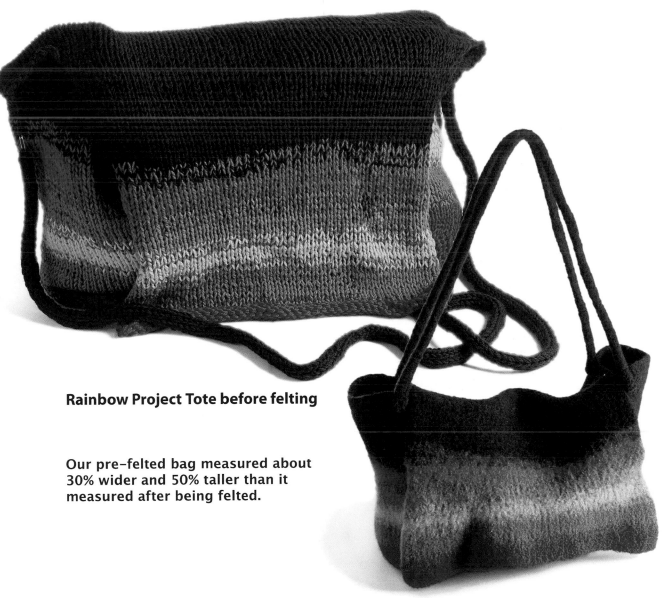

Rainbow Project Tote before felting

Our pre–felted bag measured about 30% wider and 50% taller than it measured after being felted.

Rainbow Project Tote after felting

outer edge of the pre-felted fabric, drawing the edges in.

If you find that the center of the fabric has felted as desired, but the edges are still wavy, you can continue to hand-felt the edges in the sink by rubbing vigorously with soap and hot water until they are straight.

Also, remember that since the stitches are all "locked," the edges of felted fabric can be cut if they are a bit "wavy," or if you want to make a piece a bit smaller.

When Felting Goes Awry

Sometimes felted pieces shrink too much, or become misshapen. If that happens, turn lemons into lemonade. Felt can be cut and the pieces can be used to make or decorate other projects. If the piece is large enough, use it to make placemats. Smaller pieces can be used to make trivets or coasters, just blanket stitch the edges after cutting. Felt can also be cut into appliqués which can then be sewn or dry needle felted onto purses, garments, or other projects. Be creative and have fun.

Knitting Stitch Guide

CAST ON

Leaving an end about an inch long for each stitch to be cast on, make a slip knot on the right needle.

Place the thumb and index finger of your left hand between the yarn ends with the long yarn end over your thumb, and the strand from the skein over your index finger. Close your other fingers over the strands to hold them against your palm. Spread your thumb and index fingers apart and draw the yarn into a "V."

Place the needle in front of the strand around your thumb and bring it underneath this strand. Carry the needle over and under the strand on your index finger.

Draw through loop on thumb.

Drop the loop from your thumb and draw up the strand to form a stitch on the needle.

Repeat until you have cast on the number of stitches indicated in the pattern. Remember to count the beginning slip knot as a stitch.

CABLE CAST ON

This type of cast on is used when adding stitches in the middle or at the end of a row. Make a slip knot on the left needle.

Knit a stitch in this knot and place it on the left needle.

Insert the right needle between the last two stitches on the left needle. Knit a stitch and place it on the left needle. Repeat for each stitch needed.

KNIT (K)

Insert tip of right needle from front to back in next stitch on left needle.

Bring yarn under and over the tip of the right needle.

Pull yarn loop through the stitch with right needle point.

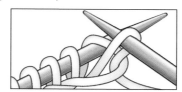

Slide the stitch off the left needle. The new stitch is on the right needle.

PURL (P)

With yarn in front, insert tip of right needle from back to front through next stitch on the left needle.

Bring yarn around the right needle counterclockwise.

With right needle, draw yarn back through the stitch.

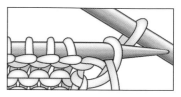

Slide the stitch off the left needle. The new stitch is on the right needle.

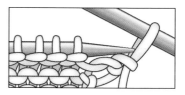

BIND OFF
Binding off (knit)

Knit first two stitches on left needle. Insert tip of left needle into first stitch worked on right needle and pull it over the second stitch and completely off the needle.

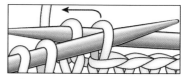

Knit the next stitch and repeat. When one stitch remains on right needle, cut yarn and draw tail through last stitch to fasten off.

Binding off (purl)

Purl first two stitches on left needle. Insert tip of left needle into first stitch worked on right needle and pull it over the second stitch and completely off the needle.

Purl the next stitch and repeat. When one stitch remains on right needle, cut

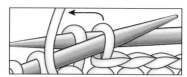

yarn and draw tail through last stitch to fasten off.

INCREASE (INC)
Two stitches in one stitch
Increase (knit)

Knit the next stitch in the usual manner, but don't remove the stitch from the left needle. Place right needle behind left needle and knit again into the back of the same stitch. Slip original stitch off left needle.

INCREASE (PURL)

Purl the next stitch in the usual manner, but don't remove the stitch from the left needle. Place right needle behind left needle and purl again into the back of the same stitch. Slip original stitch off left needle.

INVISIBLE INCREASE (M1)

There are several ways to make or increase one stitch.

Make 1 with Left Twist (M1L)

Insert left needle from front to back under the horizontal loop between the last stitch worked and next stitch on left needle.

With right needle, knit into the back of this loop.

To make this increase on the purl side, insert left needle in same manner and purl into the back of the loop.

Make 1 with Right Twist (M1R)

Insert left needle from back to front under the horizontal loop between the last stitch worked and next stitch on left needle.

With right needle, knit into the front of this loop.

To make this increase on the purl side, insert left needle in same manner and purl into the front of the loop.

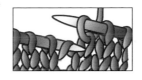

Make 1 with Backward Loop over the right needle

With your thumb, make a loop over the right needle.

Slip the loop from your thumb onto the needle and pull to tighten.

Make 1 in top of stitch below

Insert tip of right needle into the stitch on left needle one row below.

Knit this stitch; then knit the stitch on the left needle.

DECREASE (DEC)
Knit 2 together (k2tog)

Put tip of right needle through next two stitches on left needle as to knit. Knit these two stitches as one.

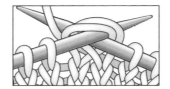

Purl 2 together (p2tog)

Put tip of right needle through next two stitches on left needle as to purl. Purl these two stitches as one.

SLIP, SLIP, KNIT (SSK)

Slip next two stitches, one at a time, as to knit from left needle to right needle.

Insert left needle in front of both stitches and work off needle together.

Slip, Slip, Purl (ssp)

Slip next two stitches, one at a time, as to knit from left needle to right needle. Slip these stitches back onto left needle keeping them twisted.

Purl these two stitches together through back loops.

Crochet Stitch Guide

CROCHET HOOKS

Metric	US	Metric	US
.60mm	14	3.00mm	D/3
.75mm	12	3.50mm	E/4
1.00mm	10	4.00mm	F/5
1.50mm	6	4.50mm	G/6
1.75mm	5	5.00mm	H/8
2.00mm	B/1	5.50mm	I/9
2.50mm	C/2	6.00mm	J/10

Chain—ch: Yo, pull through lp on hook.

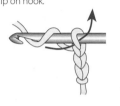

Slip stitch—sl st: Insert hook in st, yo, pull through both lps on hook.

Front loop—front lp
Back loop—back lp

Front Loop   Back Loop

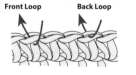

Single crochet—sc: Insert hook in st, yo, pull through st, yo, pull through both lps on hook.

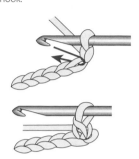

Reverse single crochet—reverse sc: Working from left to right, insert hook in next st, complete as sc.

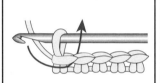

Front post stitch—fp: Back post stitch—bp: When working post st, insert hook from right to left around post st on previous row.

Back   Front

Post of Stitch

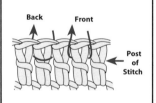

Half double crochet—hdc: Yo, insert hook in st, yo, pull through st, yo, pull through all 3 lps on hook.

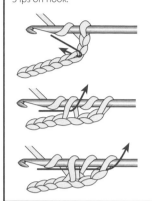

Double crochet—dc: Yo, insert hook in st, yo, pull through st, [yo, pull through 2 lps] twice.

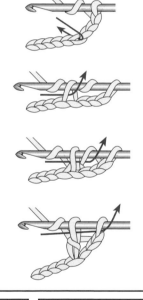

Change colors: Drop first color; with second color, pull through last 2 lps of st.

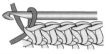

Treble crochet—tr: Yo twice, insert hook in st, yo, pull through st, [yo, pull through 2 lps] 3 times.

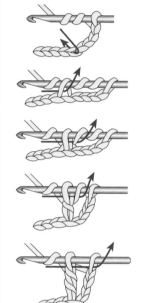

Double treble crochet—dtr: Yo 3 times, insert hook in st, yo, pull through st, [yo, pull through 2 lps] 4 times.

Single crochet decrease (sc dec): (Insert hook, yo, draw up a lp) in each of the sts indicated, yo, draw through all lps on hook.

Example of 2-sc dec

Half double crochet decrease (hdc dec): (Yo, insert hook, yo, draw lp through) in each of the sts indicated, yo, draw through all lps on hook.

Example of 2-hdc dec

Double crochet decrease (dc dec): (Yo, insert hook, yo, draw lp through, yo, draw through 2 lps on hook) in each of the sts indicated, yo, draw through all lps on hook.

Example of 2-dc dec

US		UK
sl st (slip stitch)	=	sc (single crochet)
sc (single crochet)	=	dc (double crochet)
hdc (half double crochet)	=	htr (half treble crochet)
dc (double crochet)	=	tr (treble crochet)
tr (treble crochet)	=	dtr (double treble crochet)
dtr (double treble crochet)	=	ttr (triple treble crochet)
skip	=	miss

General Information

3-Needle Bind Off

Use this technique for seaming two edges together, such as when joining a shoulder seam. Hold the edge stitches on two separate needles with right sides together.

With a third needle, knit together a stitch from the front needle with one from the back.

Repeat, knitting a stitch from the front needle with one from the back needle once more.

Slip the first stitch over the second.

Repeat knitting, a front and back pair of stitches together, then bind one off.

Fringe

Cut a piece of cardboard half as long as specified in instructions for strands plus ½ inch for trimming. Wind yarn loosely and evenly around cardboard. When cardboard is filled, cut yarn across one end. Do this several times; then begin fringing. Wind additional strands as necessary.

Single Knot Fringe

Hold specified number of strands for one knot together, fold in half. Hold project to be fringed with right side facing you. Use crochet hook to draw folded end through space or stitch indicated from right to wrong side.

Pull loose ends through folded section. Draw knot up firmly. Space knots as indicated in pattern instructions.

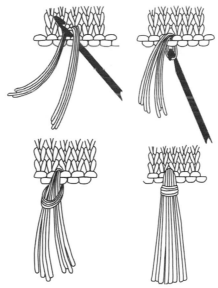

Single Knot Fringe

Double Knot Fringe

Begin by working Single Knot Fringe completely across one end of piece. With right side facing you and working from left to right, take half the strands of one knot and half the strands of the knot next to it and knot them together.

Double Knot Fringe

Triple Knot Fringe

Work Double Knot Fringe across. On the right side, work from left to right tying a third row of knots.

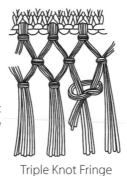

Triple Knot Fringe

Spaghetti Fringe

Following Single Knot Fringe instructions, tie each knot with just one strand of yarn.

Kitchener Stitch

This method of weaving with two needles is used for the toes of socks and flat seams. To weave the edges together and form an unbroken line of stockinette stitch, divide all stitches evenly onto two knitting needles—one behind the other. Thread yarn into tapestry needle. Hold needles with wrong sides together and work from right to left as follows:

Step 1: Insert tapestry needle into first stitch on  front needle as to purl. Draw yarn through stitch, leaving stitch on knitting needle.

Step 2: Insert tapestry needle into the first stitch on the back needle as to 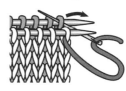 purl. Draw yarn through stitch and slip stitch off knitting needle.

Step 3: Insert tapestry needle into the next stitch on same (back) needle as to  knit, leaving stitch on knitting needle.

Step 4: Insert tapestry needle into the first stitch on the front needle as 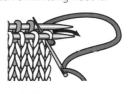 to knit. Draw yarn through stitch and slip stitch off knitting needle.

Step 5: Insert tapestry needle into the next stitch on same (front)  needle as to purl. Draw yarn through stitch, leaving stitch on knitting needle.

Repeat Steps 2 through 5 until one stitch is left on each needle. Then repeat Steps 2 and 4. Fasten off. Woven stitches should be the same size as adjacent knitted stitches.

General Information

Standard Abbreviations

[ ] work instructions within brackets as many times as directed

( ) work instructions within parentheses in the place directed

** repeat instructions following the asterisks as directed

* repeat instructions following the single asterisk as directed

" inch(es)

approx approximately

beg begin/beginning

CC contrasting color

ch chain stitch

cm centimeter(s)

cn cable needle

dec decrease/decreases/decreasing

dpn(s) double-pointed needle(s)

g gram

inc increase/increases/increasing

k knit

k²tog knit 2 stitches together

LH left hand

lp(s) loop(s)

m meter(s)

M1 make one stitch

MC main color

mm millimeter(s)

oz ounce(s)

p purl

pat(s) pattern(s)

p²tog purl 2 stitches together

psso pass slipped stitch over

psso² pass 2 slipped stitches over

rem remain/remaining

rep repeat(s)

rev St st reverse Stockinette stitch

RH right hand

rnd(s) rounds

RS right side

skp slip, knit, pass stitch over—one stitch decreased

sk²p slip 1, knit 2 together, pass slip stitch over the knit 2 together—two stitches decreased

sl slip

sl ¹k slip 1 knitwise

sl ¹p slip 1 purlwise

sl st slip stitch(es)

ssk slip, slip, knit these 2 stitches together—a decrease

st(s) stitch(es)

St st stockinette stitch/stocking stitch

tbl through back loop(s)

tog together

WS wrong side

wyib with yarn in back

wyif with yarn in front

yd(s) yard(s)

yfwd yarn forward

yo yarn over

Skill Levels

BEGINNER

Projects for first-time knitters using basic knit and purl stitches. Minimal shaping.

EASY

Projects using basic stitches, repetitive stitch patterns, simple color changes and simple shaping and finishing.

INTERMEDIATE

Projects with a variety of stitches, such as basic cables and lace, simple intarsia, double-pointed needles and knitting in the round needle techniques, mid-level shaping and finishing.

EXPERIENCED

Projects using advanced techniques and stitches, such as short rows, Fair Isle, more intricate intarsia, cables, lace patterns and numerous color changes.

Glossary

bind off—used to finish an edge

cast on—process of making foundation stitches used in knitting

decrease—means of reducing the number of stitches in a row

increase—means of adding to the number of stitches in a row

intarsia—method of knitting a multicolored pattern into the fabric

knitwise—insert needle into stitch as if to knit

make 1—method of increasing using the strand between the last stitch worked and the next stitch

place marker—placing a purchased marker or loop of contrasting yarn onto the needle for ease in working a pattern repeat

purlwise—insert needle into stitch as if to purl

right side—side of garment or piece that will be seen when worn

selvage stitch—edge stitch used to make seaming easier

slip, slip, knit—method of decreasing by moving stitches from left needle to right needle and working them together

slip stitch—an unworked stitch slipped from left needle to right needle, usually as if to purl

wrong side—side that will be inside when garment is worn

work even—continue to work in the pattern as established without working any increases or decreases

work in pattern as established—continue to work following the pattern stitch as it has been set up or established on the needle, working any increases or decreases in such a way that the established pattern remains the same

yarn over—method of increasing by wrapping the yarn over the right needle without working a stitch

General Information

INCHES INTO MILLIMETERS & CENTIMETERS (Rounded off slightly)

inches	mm	cm	inches	cm	inches	cm	inches	cm
1/8	3	0.3	5	12.5	21	53.5	38	96.5
1/4	6	0.6	5 1/2	14	22	56	39	99
3/8	10	1	6	15	23	58.5	40	101.5
1/2	13	1.3	7	18	24	61	41	104
5/8	15	1.5	8	20.5	25	63.5	42	106.5
3/4	20	2	9	23	26	66	43	109
7/8	22	2.2	10	25.5	27	68.5	44	112
1	25	2.5	11	28	28	71	45	114.5
1 1/4	32	3.2	12	30.5	29	73.5	46	117
1 1/2	38	3.8	13	33	30	76	47	119.5
1 3/4	45	4.5	14	35.5	31	79	48	122
2	50	5	15	38	32	81.5	49	124.5
2 1/2	65	6.5	16	40.5	33	84	50	127
3	75	7.5	17	43	34	86.5		
3 1/2	90	9	18	46	35	89		
4	100	10	19	48.5	36	91.5		
4 1/2	115	11.5	20	51	37	94		

KNITTING NEEDLES CONVERSION CHART

U.S.	0	1	2	3	4	5	6	7	8	9	10	10 1/2	11	13	15
Metric(mm)	2	2 1/4	2 3/4	3 1/4	3 1/2	3 3/4	4	4 1/2	5	5 1/2	6	6 1/2	8	9	10

CROCHET HOOKS CONVERSION CHART

U.S.	1/B	2/C	3/D	4/E	5/F	6/G	8/H	9/I	10/J	10½/K	N
Continental-mm	2.25	2.75	3.25	3.5	3.75	4.25	5	5.5	6	6.5	9.0

Standard Yarn Weight System

Categories of yarn, gauge ranges, and recommended needle sizes

Yarn Weight Symbol & Category Names	1 SUPER FINE	2 FINE	3 LIGHT	4 MEDIUM	5 BULKY	6 SUPER BULKY
Type of Yarns in Category	Sock, Fingering, Baby	Sport, Baby	DK, Light Worsted	Worsted, Afghan, Aran	Chunky, Craft, Rug	Bulky, Roving
Knit Gauge* Ranges in Stockinette Stitch to 4 inches	21–32 sts	23–26 sts	21–24 sts	16–20 sts	12–15 sts	6–11 sts
Recommended Needle in Metric Size Range	2.25–3.25mm	3.25–3.75mm	3.75–4.5mm	4.5–5.5mm	5.5–8mm	8mm
Recommended Needle U.S. Size Range	1 to 3	3 to 5	5 to 7	7 to 9	9 to 11	11 and larger

* GUIDELINES ONLY: The above reflect the most commonly used gauges and needle sizes for specific yarn categories.

Special Thanks

WE WOULD LIKE TO THANK PLYMOUTH YARN CO. FOR PROVIDING ALL THE YARN USED IN THIS BOOK. WE REALLY APPRECIATE THE HELP PROVIDED BY THEIR STAFF, ESPECIALLY JOANNE TURCOTTE, THROUGHOUT THE PUBLISHING PROCESS. IT'S BEEN GREAT WORKING WITH THEM. WE ALSO THANK THE TALENTED DESIGNERS WHOSE WORK IS FEATURED IN THIS COLLECTION.